# MEDICAL JOKES & HUMOUR

**FOR ADULTS ONLY**

Clifford Sawhney

*Published by:*

F-2/16, Ansari road, Daryaganj, New Delhi-110002
☎ 23240026, 23240027 • *Fax:* 011-23240028
*Email:* info@vspublishers.com • *Website:* www.vspublishers.com

**Regional Office : Hyderabad**
5-1-707/1, Brij Bhawan (Beside Central Bank of India Lane)
Bank Street, Koti, Hyderabad - 500 095
☎ 040-24737290
*E-mail:* vspublishershyd@gmail.com

**Branch Office : Mumbai**
☎ 022-23510736
*E-mail* vspublishersmum@gmail.com

Follow us on:

All books available at **www.vspublishers.com**

© Copyright: V&S PUBLISHERS
ISBN 978-93-813848-6-2
Edition : 2015

---

The Copyright of this book, as well as all matter contained herein (including illustrations) rests with the Publisher. No person shall copy the name of the book, its title design, matter and illustrations in any form and in any language, totally or partially or in any form. Anybody doing so shall face legal action and will be responsible for damages.

---

*Printed at :* Param Offseters Okhla New Delhi-110020

## DEDICATION

This book is dedicated to my eclectic and ecumenical upbringing, which taught me that the only thing that counts at the end of the day is a good laugh and the Truth.

## Preface

Medical Jokes & Humour focuses on the non-vegetarian variety, since this is precisely what most adults want, although they may say just the opposite in polite company! If the bold and the bawdy offends you easily, we suggest you drop this book like a hot potato.

Having said that, we realise that despite any moral predisposition, you will be all the more tempted to read this! Please do so without reservations – the ensuing bouts of laughter will wash out all trace of toxic characteristics (such as hypocrisy, double standards and negativity) from the body. Besides, to tell the truth, the purpose of warning prudes to drop the book is to ensure they do otherwise!

With this statutory warning having been served to readers, those who proceed across these delectable pages would not mind some risque comments and barbs. And for those who still do mind, never mind!

—Clifford Sawhney

## Acknowledgements

This book has been compiled from various sources, including individual raconteurs, with the actual creators of the jokes largely faceless and unknown, some having long since left for the happy hunting grounds. To one and all of these masters of humour, my sincere thanks.

# Contents

1. Nurses For Courses ......................................... 7
2. General Practitioner's Blues .......................... 10
3. The Patient Syndrome.................................... 31
4. Chemists: Over-the-counter Fun ..................... 34
5. Dental Drills................................................... 42
6. Multiple Practitioners' Shenanigans ............... 46
7. The Surgeon's Special .................................... 54
8. Psychiatric Feedback ..................................... 65
9. Gynaecological Openings................................ 78
10. Obstetrician's Day.......................................... 83
11. Sex Therapists' Tricks.................................... 89
12. Viagra Tales ................................................. 104
13. AIDS ............................................................ 109
14. Vet Antics.................................................... 111
15. Optical Illusions .......................................... 114
16. Doctors' Mixed Bag ...................................... 116
17. Merry Old Men ............................................. 130
18. Medical Limericks........................................ 137
19. The World of Assorted Medical Cracks......... 142
20. Short Medical Insights ................................ 157
21. The Ultimate Medical Glossary .................... 165

# Nurses For Courses

## The Tight Experience

An old man in a nursing home is hornier than Chunky Pandey ever was. So when he sees this nurse who is well endowed on all fronts, he coos, "How about a quickie for twenty bucks?"

The nurse too is as randy as hell and will have anything on two feet or four. She agrees and gets on top of the old man. They have a ball for about ten minutes.

After the act, having enjoyed the 'tight' experience, the old man says, "What the heck, if I knew you were a virgin, I would have paid you a hundred bucks."

The nurse smiles sweetly and replies, "And if I knew you could get it up that high, I would have taken off my panties!"

## The Hole Joke

There was this arrogant jerk of a doctor who had four nurses working under him. So on April 1, 2002, each of the nurses played a practical prank on him. Later that night, during their break, they were all discussing the fast one each had pulled on the doctor.

The first nurse said, "I stuffed cotton in his stethoscope so he couldn't hear."

The second nurse said, "I let the mercury out of his thermometer and painted them all to read 106 degrees."

The third nurse said, "Well, I did better than the two of you. I poked holes in all the condoms that he keeps in his desk drawer."

Hearing this, the fourth nurse fainted.

## Back-to-Front Operations

Two doctors in practice in a small-town clinic had to hire a new nurse when the one they had won the Zee online lottery and quit. They interviewed Nurse Shilpa and decided to hire her. She had only worked a couple of days when one doctor called the other to his office and said they would have to terminate Nurse Shilpa's services.

"Why, we just hired her?"

"Well, I think she is dyslexic and gets things backward. I told her to give Mr Dandekar two shots of morphine every 24 hours, but she gave him 24 shots in two hours and it almost killed him. I told her to give Mrs Holkar an enema every 12 hours and she gave her 12 in one hour."

The doctor had barely finished outlining his reasons when the other doctor rushed out of the room. "Where are you going in such a tearing hurry?" the doctor inquired.

"To see Nurse Shilpa – I had just instructed her to prick Mr Muthu's boil!"

## Carnal Shot

A big-shot businessman has to spend a couple of days in the hospital. He is a royal pain in the you-know-where to the nurses because he throws his weight around with them just like with his employees.

Within hours, the hospital staff wants to be miles away from him. The head nurse is the only one who can stand up to the jerk. Coming into his room, she announces, "I have to take your temperature."

He cribs for several minutes, but finally settles down, crosses his arms and opens his mouth.

"No, I'm sorry," the nurse states, deadpan, "but for this reading, I cannot use an oral thermometer."

This sparks another round of complaining, but eventually he rolls over and bares his rear end. After feeling the nurse insert the thermometer, he hears her announce, "I have to get something. Now you stay JUST LIKE THAT until I get back!"

She leaves the door to his room open on her way out. He curses under his breath as he hears people walking past his door laughing. After almost an hour, the man's doctor comes into the room. "What's going on here?" demands the doctor.

Angrily, the man answers, "What's the matter, doc? Haven't you ever seen someone having their temperature taken?"

After a pregnant pause, the doctor confesses, "Well, no. I guess I haven't. Not with a carnation anyway!"

## Nursery Lines

Did you hear about the nurse who swallowed a razor blade?

She gave herself a tonsillectomy, an appendectomy, a hysterectomy, and circumcised three of the doctors on her shift!

Interns think of God, residents pray to God, doctors talk to God, nurses ARE God.

There was once a guy whose tongue was so long that when he stuck it out for the doctor, the nurse went, "Aaaaaahhh!!!"

The nurse who can smile when things go wrong is probably going off duty.

# General Practitioner's Blues

## Utterly Depressing

A depressed man goes to the doctor. "Doctorsaab," he says, "I'm terribly depressed. Life seems harsh and cruel. There is no laughter in my life. I feel I'm totally alone in this big bad world, trying to keep the show going."

The doctor is busy reading his notes and does not bother to look up, but responds: "No probs. The treatment is very simple. You need a change of scene. Something light and hilarious… The great comedian Johnny Lever is going to be in town for one week tomorrow onwards. Go and see one of his shows. That should have you dying with laughter."

On hearing this piece of advice, the man bursts into uncontrollable sobs just as the doctor looks up: "But doctor… I am Johnny Lever!"

## Daily Change

A woman goes to her doctor complaining that she is exhausted all the time. After the diagnostic tests show nothing, the doctor gets around to asking her how often she has intercourse.

"Every Monday to Saturday," she says.

The doctor advises her to cut out Wednesday. "I can't," says the woman. "That's the only night I'm at home with my husband."

## The Busy Doc

A young doctor was just setting up his first clinic when his secretary told him there was a man to see him. The doctor wanted to make a good first impression by having the man think he was very busy. He told his secretary to show the man in.

At that moment, the doctor picked up the telephone and pretended to be having a conversation with a patient. The man waited until the "conversation" was over. Then, the doctor put the telephone down and asked, "Can I help you?"

"No! I'm just here to connect your telephone," replied the man coolly.

## Frog Trick

A man goes into the doctor's clinic with a frog stuck to his forehead. The startled doctor asks, "How did that happen?"

The frog replies, "It started as a boil on my bum!"

## 24-Hour Countdown

Doctor: "I have some bad news and some very bad news."

Patient: "Well, you can give me the bad news first."

Doctor: "The lab submitted your test report yesterday. They said you have only 24 hours to live."

Patient: "Only 24 hours! That's terrible! What could be worse? What's the very bad news?"

Doctor: "Well, I've been trying to contact you since yesterday!"

## Problematic Problem

Patient: "Doctor, help! I have a serious memory problem. I can't remember anything!"

Doctor: "Oh I see! Since when do you have this problem?"

Patient: "Problem? What problem?"

☺  ❖  ☺

## Orgasmic Delight

Patient: "Doctor, you must help me. Every time I sneeze, I have an orgasm."

Doctor: "Really! What have you been doing about it?"

Patient, grinning: "Oh, nothing much. Simply taking snuff!"

☺  ❖  ☺

## Healthy Problem

Patient: "Doctor, I have a strange problem. I feel unhealthy and depressed."

Doctor: "You should cut down on drinks."

Patient: "But doctor, I don't touch a drop!"

Doctor: "You should cut down on smoking."

Patient: "Doctor, I don't smoke!"

Doctor: "You should stop taking drugs."

Patient: "I don't ever set my eyes on drugs."

Doctor: "You should cut down on womanising."

Patient: "I haven't touched a woman in my life even with a barge pole."

Doctor, exasperated: "Ah, that's your problem! You never do anything! So go get yourself a drink, learn to smoke, enjoy drugs, and find a couple of girlfriends!"

☺  ❖  ☺

## Fighting Fit

Patient: "Doctor, what I need is something to stir me up; something to put me in a fighting mood; something to make me fighting fit. Did you write down something like that in this prescription?"

Doctor: "Oh, don't bother about this. My bill will do all that!"

## Soft Bone

Doctor: "Did you know that there are more than 1,000 bones in the human body?"

Raghu: "Shhh, doctor, softly! My dog's outside in the waiting room!"

## Doctor-speak

Doctor to patient: "Congratulations, Mr Muthuswami! You're in great shape for a man of 60. Too bad you're only 40!"

## Crap Talk

Patient: "Doctor, you've got to help me. I eat apples, apples later come out in the toilet. I eat bananas, bananas come out. I eat grapes, grapes come out... How do I cure this problem to pass normal stool?"

Doctor: "That should pose no problem at all. Simply eat shit!"

## Prison Tales

Prisoner: "Look here, doc! You've already removed my spleen, tonsils, adenoids, and one of my kidneys. I only came here to see if you could get me out of this place!"

Doctor: "I am, I am. Bit by bit, bit by bit!"

## Driving Tests

Smita: "I get terribly nervous and frightened during driving tests!"

Doctor: "Never mind. You'll pass eventually."

Smita: "No, you don't understand! I'm the examiner!"

☺   ❖   ☺

## Only 80

Doctor: "Don't worry, Mr Buddhadev. You're in good health. You'll live to be 80."

Buddhadev: "But doctor, I am 80 right now!"

Doctor: "See? Didn't I tell you so!"

☺   ❖   ☺

## Sobering Thought

The doctor completed an examination of the patient, shaking his head ruefully: "I can't find a cause for your complaint. Frankly, I think it's due to drinking."

"In that case," says the sympathetic patient, "I'll come back when you're sober."

☺   ❖   ☺

## Pissed Off

A man walks into a crowded doctor's clinic. As he approaches the desk, the receptionist asks, "Yes sir, may we help you?"

"There's something wrong with my dick," he replies.

The receptionist is aggravated and says, "You shouldn't come into a crowded clinic and say things like that."

"Why not? You asked me what was wrong and I told you!" he says.

"We do not use language like that here," she says. "Please go outside and come back in and say that there's something wrong with your ear or whatever."

The man walks out, waits for several minutes and re-enters. The receptionist smiles smugly and asks, "Yes sir?"

"There's something wrong with my ear," the man states.

The receptionist nods approvingly. "And what is wrong with your ear, sir?"

"I can't piss out of it!" the man hisses.

## Slow-motion Flashback

"How did this happen?" the doctor asks the middle-aged farmhand as he sets the man's broken leg.

"Well, doc, 25 years ago..."

"Never mind the past. Tell me how you broke your leg this morning."

"Like I was saying... 25 years ago, when I first started working on the farm, that night, right after I'd gone to bed, the farmer's beautiful daughter came into my room. She asked me if there was anything I wanted. I said, 'No, everything is fine.' 'Are you sure?' she asked. 'I'm sure,' I said. 'Isn't there anything I can do for you?' she wanted to know. 'I think not,' I replied."

"Excuse me," says the irritated doctor, "what does this 25-year-old story have to do with your leg?"

"Well, this morning," the farmhand explains with a shrug, "when it dawned on me what she meant, I fell off the roof!"

## Television Sex

A woman goes to her doctor complaining of bad knee pains. After the diagnostic tests show nothing, the doctor questions her, "There must be something you're doing that you haven't told me. Can you think of anything that might be doing this to your knees?"

"Well," she says a little sheepishly, "my husband and I have sex doggie-style on the floor every night."

"That's got to be it," says the doctor. "There are plenty of other positions and ways to have sex, you know."

"Not if you're watching TV at the same time!" she replies.

## Cat-n-Mouse Game

A man swallows a mouse while sleeping on the couch one day. His wife quickly calls the doctor and says, "Doctor, please come quickly. My husband just swallowed a mouse and he's gagging and thrashing about."

"I'll be right over," the doctor hastily reassures her. "In the meantime, keep waving a piece of cheese over his mouth to try to attract the mouse out of there."

When the doctor arrives, he sees the wife waving a piece of fried fish over her husband's mouth. "Uhh, I told you to use cheese, not fried fish, to lure the mouse."

"I know, doc," she replies, "but first I've got to get the stupid cat out of him!"

☺ ❖ ☺

## Animal Fare

There was a village doctor who was the only practitioner for miles around. One day, he wanted to go on a fishing trip so he called the vet and asked him to look after things while he was gone. The vet asked, "Is anything happening?"

The doctor replied, "Mrs Nagwekar is almost due, but I don't think the baby will come before I get back. Anyway, if it does, just deliver it. This is her third and the first two went really easily."

The vet said, "Okay!" and the doctor went on the fishing trip.

When he returned, he called the vet. "How did things go while I was gone?"

"Pretty good."

"Did Mrs Nagwekar have her baby?"

"Yes, it was an 8-pound boy. Everyone's doing fine."

"Did you have any trouble?"

"Well, there was just one little problem."

"What was that?"

"I had a terrible time getting her to eat the afterbirth!"

## An ecnalubmA

The doctor began his examination of an elderly man by asking what brought him to the hospital.

Said the man, with a deadpan expression, "An ambulance."

## Oral Service

Ahfat and Musibat are walking through a Rajasthan desert. Suddenly, a snake bites Ahfat's prick! "AAIIIIIII!!" he screams, and Musibat panics.

"What can we do?"

"We should call a doctor."

WHAMMM! Suddenly, in the middle of the desert, there's a telephone booth. Musibat goes in and calls a doctor. TRING, TRING! TRING, TRING! Musibat: "My friend was bitten by a snake. What should we do?"

Doctor: "What kind of snake?"

Musibat: "A one-metre, green-yellow one."

Doctor: "Accha, Accha. Those are very dangerous."

Musibat: "What can we do?"

Doctor: "The only thing you can do is to suck the poison out. Otherwise, your friend will be dead within half an hour."

Musibat hangs up and goes out of the telephone booth. Ahfat, pale as night, asks what the doctor said.

Musibat: "Too bad, you'll be dead within half an hour."

☺   ❖   ☺

## Hair Trouble

A woman went to her doctor for a follow-up visit after the doctor had prescribed the male hormone, testosterone, for her. She was a little worried about some of the side effects she was experiencing. "Doctor, the hormones you've been giving me have really helped, but I'm afraid that you're giving me too much. I've started growing hair in places that I've never grown hair before."

The doctor reassured her. "A little hair growth is a perfectly normal side effect of testosterone. Just where has this hair appeared?"

"On my testicles!"

☺   ❖   ☺

## A-cute Angina

This young couple had only been married for about two weeks when the wife complains of a burning sensation in her chest. She tells her husband, who suggests that she go to the doctor to be examined. She arranges an appointment and goes the following day.

While at work, the husband receives a call from the doctor. Doctor: "I have to inform you that your wife has acute angina..."

Husband: "I know, I know. She's also got a nice pair of breasts too!"

☺   ❖   ☺

## Late Mate

Mr Latelatif had this problem of getting up late in the morning and was always late for work. His boss was mad at him and threatened to fire him if he didn't do something about it. So Latelatif went to his doctor who gave him a pill and told him to take it before he went to bed.

Latelatif slept well and actually beat the alarm in the morning. He had a leisurely breakfast and drove cheerfully to work. "Boss," he said, "the pill actually worked!"

"That's all fine," said the agitated boss. "But where were you yesterday?"

## Communist Dilemma

This was in the days of Comrade Brezhnev and much before Comrade Gorbachev came along and screwed the Soviet Union inside out. Dmitri walks into the Moscow health clinic and asks to see a ear-and-eye doctor. The nurse explains that there isn't a specialist in those two areas at the clinic, but they do have an eye doctor AND a ear, nose and throat specialist. She further goes on to suggest, after seeing his rather vacant stare, that he see the ENT specialist and, if that doesn't work, why, he can then go to the ophthalmologist.

So a month later (remember, the clinic is run by the Soviet bureaucracy) he is shown to the doc's office. The following dialogue ensues. Doctor: "So, tell me, Comrade Dmitri. What seems to be the trouble?"

Dmitri: "Doc! Doc! You got to help me! I'm going crazy!"

Doctor: "Just calm down and tell me your symptoms."

Dmitri: "Well, I... OK. I... I'll try. It's like my ears and my eyeballs aren't connected to the same man. I can't see what I hear, and I can't hear what I see!"

At this, the doctor sighs, shakes his head, closes his notebook, and prepares for his next patient. When Dmitri asks what he's doing, he explains: "Really, I'm very sorry, Comrade Dmitri. But there's no known cure for Communism."

## Missing Cookie

Mr Haddi Pasli went to a doctor because he was losing weight. Haddi Pasli found out he had a tapeworm, and was instructed by the doctor to bring a doughnut, a pastry and a cookie with him on his next visit. When he was being examined the doctor shoved the doughnut, pastry and, finally, the cookie up Haddi Pasli's rear. Haddi Pasli protested, but the doctor calmed him down, saying it was part of the therapy.

This treatment continued for several weeks and every time the doctor shoved a doughnut, a pastry and a cookie up his butt. Finally, after many visits, the doctor instructed Haddi Pasli to bring a doughnut, a pastry and a hammer for the next visit.

D-day arrived and this time the doctor shoved only the doughnut and the pastry up Haddi Pasli's posterior. After a few minutes, the furious tapeworm appeared out of his a***hole and demanded, "Where's my cookie?!"

WHAM!!! Down came the doctor's arm with the hammer in tow!

## Good Heavens...

A doctor dies and goes to heaven. St Peter meets him at the Pearly Gates and checks him in. After he's registered, St Peter tells him, "Look at the time: you must be hungry! Heaven Cafeteria is serving lunch, why don't you get yourself something to eat?"

The doctor goes to the cafeteria and notices the long queue. He immediately sneaks in at the front, only to hear loud protests. "I'm a doctor," he says. "I'm a busy man. I don't have time to wait in line."

The others say, "You're in heaven now, we're all the same here; get to the back of the line and wait your turn!"

A few weeks later, waiting patiently in line for lunch, the doctor notices a man come dashing in, wearing scrubs and a lab coat, stethoscope around his neck. He butts in at the head of the line and no one utters a squeak.

"Hey!" the doctor says to the guy in front of him. "Who does that guy think he is?"

"Oh, that's God," says the guy. "He likes to pretend he's a doctor."

## Patriotic Indian

A man goes to the doctor for a check-up. After the check-up, the doctor tells the man he has bad news. "You only have six months to live."

The man sits for a while thinking, and then says, "There's only one thing I can do. I'm going to become a Pakistani."

The doctor is taken aback. "You've been a patriotic Indian all your life. Why do you want to become a Pakistani now?"

The man smirks, "Better one of them dies than one of us!"

## Coming Again

A doctor and his wife were having a big argument at breakfast. "You aren't so good in bed either!" he shouted and stormed off to work.

By afternoon, he decided he'd better make amends and phoned home. After many rings, his wife picked up the phone. "What took you so long to answer?"

"I was in bed."

"What were you doing in bed this late?"

"Getting a second opinion."

## Double Trouble

A patient goes to his doctor, a Sardarji. Patient: "I am having a hard time hearing. I cannot even hear myself cough."

Doctor: "Here is a prescription. Take the medicine for seven days, then return for a check-up."

Seven days later. Patient: "Thanks a million, doctor. At least, I can hear myself cough now. So what did you do to make me hear better?"

Doctor: "Not much. I gave you medicines that increased your cough!"

## Eighty-eight

A woman went to her new doctor for a check-up. He turned out to be absolutely gorgeous! He told her he was going to put his hand on her back and wanted her to say "Eighty-eight".

"Eighty-eight," she purred.

"Good. Now I'm going to put my hand on your throat and I want you to again say 'Eighty-eight.'"

"Eighhty... eighhhhtttt."

"Fine. Now I'm going to put my hand on your chest and I want you one more time to say 'Eighty-eight.'"

"One, two, three, four, five..." the lady counted.

## The Doc's Here

An accident had just taken place, when a woman stepped forward and prepared to help the victim. Suddenly, she was asked to step aside by a man who announced, "Step back please! I've had a course in first aid and I'm trained in mouth-to-mouth resuscitation."

The woman watched his procedures for a few moments and then tapped him on the shoulder. "When you get to the part about calling a doctor," she said, "don't bother. I'm already here."

## Again and Again

At a major medical convention, the internist arises to announce that he has discovered a new miracle antibiotic.

"What's it cure?" asks a member of the audience.

"Nothing we don't already have a drug for," the internist replies.

"Well, what's so miraculous about it?"

"One of the side effects is short-term memory loss. Several of my patients have paid my bill three or four times!" chuckles the internist.

## Hear, Hear

A man tells his family doctor: "Doc, I think my wife's going deaf."

The doctor answers, "Well, here's something you can try on her to test her hearing. Stand some distance away from her and ask her a question. If she doesn't answer, move a little closer and ask again. Keep repeating this until she answers. Then you'll be able to tell just how hard of hearing she really is."

The man goes home and tries it out. He walks in and says, "Darling, what's for dinner?" He doesn't hear an answer, so he moves closer to her. "Darling, what's for dinner?"

Still no answer! He repeats this several times, until he's standing just a few feet away from her. Finally, she answers, "For the eleventh time, I said we're having Mutton Curry!"

## Doctor's Privilege

A young small-town guy and his new bride wanted desperately to start a family, but they didn't know what they had to do to have children. So they decided to visit a doctor. With a great deal of embarrassment, the young man explained their situation. The doctor took out his charts and books for adolescents and carefully explained about the birds and the bees. The two looked at each other, bewildered, then at the doctor.

The doctor attempted to explain in various ways the ins and outs of human reproduction. Again no luck!

Thoroughly exasperated, the doctor laid the bride on the examination table, removed all her clothes and had her there and then. He then turned to the young man and asked, "Now do you understand?"

"Yes, doctor," the young man responded, "but just one question."

Slapping his forehead in total disbelief, the doctor squawked, "Yes, what is it now?"

Replied the young man, "How often do I have to bring her to you?"

## First Strike

The doctor took Dinesh into the room and said, "Dinesh, I have some good news and some bad news."

Dinesh: "Give me the good news first."

"Well, we're going to name a disease after you!"

## Improper Eating

A man walks into a doctor's office. He has a cucumber up his nose, a carrot in his left ear and a banana in his right ear. "So doc, what do you think is the matter with me?" he asks.

The doctor replies nonchalantly, "You're not eating properly."

## Second Opinion

Dukhiram walked into the doctor's office to find out the results of a series of tests that he had undergone. His worst fears were confirmed.

"I am afraid I have some bad news for you, Mr Dukhiram. You're going to die in four weeks."

Dukhiram was distraught. "Doctor, that's terrible. I want a second opinion."

"Okay. You're ugly too."

## Doctor's Message

For his wife's birthday party, a doctor ordered a cake with this inscription: "You are not getting older. You are just getting better."

Asked how he wanted the message arranged, he said, "Just put 'You are not getting older' at the top and 'You are just getting better' at the bottom."

It wasn't until the good doctor was ready to serve the cake that he discovered it read:

"YOU ARE NOT GETTING OLDER AT THE TOP,

YOU ARE JUST GETTING BETTER AT THE BOTTOM."

## Painful Finding

A Sardarji goes to his doctor (also a Sardar) and says, "You have to help me. My finger hurts wherever I touch it."

The doctor says, "Touch your nose," and the Sardar screams. The doctor says, "Touch your elbow," and the Sardar winces in pain.

The doctor finally says, "We are going to run some tests including, blood, X-rays, ECG, stress test, MRI... and then you can come back in two days."

Two days later, the Sardar comes back and says, "It still hurts wherever I touch. Did you find out what is wrong with me?"

The doctor says, "Of course, I did. You have broken your finger!"

## Seconds

"Doctor! Doctor! You have to see my wife right away! I think she has appendicitis!"

The doctor shook his head. "That's impossible! Your wife had her appendix removed last year. Have you ever seen anybody with a second appendix?"

"Doctor, have you ever seen anybody with a second wife?"

## All in the Mind

After examining the patient, Mr Dukhiparinda, the doctor told the worried wife, "No need to hospitalise him. I've checked everything possible, and he isn't really ill at all – he just thinks he's sick."

A week later, the doctor telephoned to see if Dukhiparinda was doing better.

"How's your husband today?" he asked.

"Worse," replied the wife. "Now he thinks he's dead."

## Time Tested

"Brace yourself, Mr Kapadia," the physician told the patient on whom he had performed a battery of costly tests. "You have approximately six months to live."

"But I don't have insurance, doctor," said Kapadia, "and I can't skimp and save enough to pay you in that time!"

"All right, all right," soothed the medical man. "Let's say nine months, then?"

☺ ❖ ☺

## Live Prescription

A man goes to the doctor and complains that no medicine helps with his migraines. "No trouble at all. When I have a migraine," says the doctor, "I go home and soak in a hot bath. Then I have my wife sponge me off with the hottest water I can stand, especially around the forehead. Then I take her into the bedroom, and even if my head is killing me, we have sex. Almost immediately, the headache is gone. Try it and come back in six weeks."

Six weeks later, the patient returns with a big grin. "It worked!" he exclaims. "I've had migraines for years, and no one's ever helped me before!"

"Glad to help," says the doctor.

"By the way," the patient adds, "you have a really nice house."

☺ ❖ ☺

## Back-up

The tired doctor was awakened by a phone call in the middle of the night. "Please, you have to come right over," pleaded the distraught mother. "My child has swallowed a contraceptive."

The physician dressed quickly, but before he could get out of the door, the phone rang again. "You don't have to come over after all," the woman said with a sigh of relief. "My husband just found another one."

☺ ❖ ☺

## Private Discharge

Mrs Chatterjee went to see her doctor. When he inquired about her complaint she replied that she suffered from a discharge. He instructed her to get undressed and lie down on the examining table. She did so.

The doctor put on rubber gloves and began to massage her 'private parts'. After a couple of minutes he asked, "How does that feel?"

"Wonderful!" she replied. "But the discharge is from the ear!"

## The Big Breath

A medical practitioner was examining his patient who happened to be big-breasted but hard of hearing. He put his stethoscope to her chest and said, "Big breaths."

The woman replied, "Yes, they used to be bigger!"

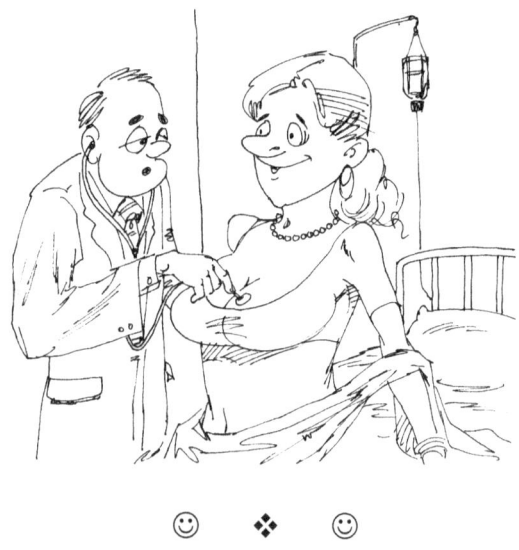

## Secret of Longevity

A man goes to the doctor and says, "Doc, I would like to live very long. What should I do?"

"I think that is a wise decision," the doctor replies. "Let's see, do you smoke?"

"Oh... Half-pack a day."

"Starting NOW, no more smoking."

The man agrees.

The doctor then asks, "Do you drink?"

"Oh, well doc, not much, just a bit of wine with my meals, and a beer or two every once in a while."

"Starting now, you drink only water. No exceptions."

The man is a bit upset, but agrees.

The doctor asks, "How much do you eat?"

"Oh, well, you know, doc, normal stuff."

"Starting now you are going on a very strict diet: you will eat only raw vegetables, with no dressing, and non-fat cottage cheese."

The man is now really worried. "Doc, is all this really necessary?"

"Do you want to live long?"

"Yes."

"Absolutely necessary! And don't even think of breaking the diet."

The man is quite restless, but the doctor continues, "Do you have sex?"

"Yeah, once a week or so... but only with my wife!" he adds hurriedly.

"As soon as you get out of here, you are going to buy twin beds. No more sex for you."

The man is appalled. "Doc, are you sure I'm going to live longer this way?"

"I have no idea, but whatever your lifespan hereafter, I assure you it will seem like an eternity!"

## Inactive Partner

While assisting in an exam on a young woman who was presented to the practitioner with lower abdominal pains, the doctor asked if she was sexually active.

The young woman appeared slightly embarrassed by the question, but replied, "No, I just lie there."

## Touch-up Artist

My doctor is wonderful. Once, when I couldn't afford an operation, he touched up my X-rays!

# The Patient Syndrome

## Glasses Please
Patient: "Doctor, I think I need glasses."

Teller: "You certainly do. This is a bank!"

## Trouble in Waiting
An artist asked the gallery owner if there had been any interest in his paintings on display at that time. "I have good news and bad news," the owner replied. "The good news is that a gentleman inquired about your work and wondered if it would appreciate in value after your death. When I told him it would, he bought all 15 of your paintings."

"That's wonderful!" the artist exclaimed. "What's the bad news?"

"Well," the gallery owner drawled, "the guy was your family doctor."

## Bolt from the Blue
Heena's husband had been slipping in and out of a coma for several months, yet she had stayed by his bedside each and every day. One day, when he regained consciousness, he motioned her to come closer.

As she sat by his side, he whispered, eyes full of tears: "You know what? You have been with me all through the bad times. When I got fired, you were there to support me. When my business failed, you were there. When I met with an accident, you were by my side. When we lost the house, you stayed right here. When my health started failing, you were still by my side. You know what?"

"What, dear?" Heena gently asked, smiling as her heart began to fill with warmth.

"I think you're bringing me bad luck!"

## The Final Warning

Three desperately ill men met their doctor one day to discuss their options. One was an alcoholic, the second a chain-smoker and the third a homosexual sex addict.

Addressing all three of them, the doctor said: "If any of you indulge in your vices one more time, you will definitely die."

The men left the doctor's office, each convinced that he would never again indulge in his vice.

While walking towards the railway station for their return trip to the suburbs, they passed a bar. The alcoholic, hearing the loud music and seeing the lights, could not stop himself. His buddies accompanied him into the bar, where he had a peg of whiskey. No sooner had he placed the glass on the bar, he fell off his stool, stone dead.

Totally shaken up, his companions left the bar, realising how seriously they must take the doctor's words.

As they walked along, they came upon a cigarette butt lying on the ground, still burning. Frantically, the homosexual looked at the chain-smoker and warned: "If you bend over to pick that up, we're both dead!"

# Chemists: Over-the-counter Fun

## Condom Suspenders

This kid walks into the chemist store and goes: "I've a hot date tonight, a sure shot where I'm going to roll in the hay. And my friends said you could fix me up for it."

"What do you want?" the chemist smiles.

"Well, it's a hot date, man. A sure shot! You know...." the kid whispers sheepishly.

"What do you want?" the chemist repeats patiently.

"I need some protection, okay!" the flustered kid replies.

"What size?"

"Size? Hell, I don't know anything about size... Whatever is considered average I guess," the kid blurts.

"That'll be 30 bucks, including tax."

"Tacks? What tacks? I thought condoms stayed on by themselves!"

## The H-O-T Date

A 16-year-old teenager has a hot date with a girl, so he goes to the chemist to buy some condoms. The chemist asks, "What can I do for you?"

The teenager looks around hurriedly and hesitantly says, "I'd like to... er... ah... buy a condom."

The chemist puts a box of condoms on the counter and says, "Okay. Here you are."

Thinking that this was rather easy and painless, the teenager says, "Well, now that I think about it, I'm sure I'll be needing two boxes of condoms."

The chemist hands him another one and replies, "Well, okay?"

Getting even bolder, the teenager then says, "Actually, it's a pretty hot date I have tonight. I think I'll be needing four boxes of condoms!"

The kid finally leaves with six boxes of condoms!

Later that night, the teenager arrives at his girlfriend's house. She tells him that he's invited to stay for dinner. So he goes in and sits down at the table with her entire family. The father asks if he'd like to say grace before beginning the meal.

The teenager quickly agrees to say the prayer and begins, "Oh Lord, thanks a ton for this food and the hands that made it, and the farmers who took the time to grow it and...."

This goes on for nearly 10 minutes, with the kid blessing everything – including the table, the silverware, all the containers, the floor...

Amazed, the girl finally turns to her boyfriend and says, "Gosh! I didn't know you were really soooooo religious."

The mortified boy whispers back, "And I didn't know your father was a chemist!"

## The Poetic Assistant

A young lad starts working at a chemist store. The owner is explaining the rudiments of the job to the youth... "When customers come into the store, be very polite with them and try to put a little poetry into it when you're talking to them." The youth can't figure out what the chemist means by this, so the latter says that he should observe when the next customer comes in and watch how s/he is dealt with.

A little later, a middle-aged woman comes and asks for something for a tummy problem. The chemist says, "There's a lot of that virus going about, but this pink mixture should sort you out!"

"Oh thank you very much!" says the middle-aged woman and leaves the store.

So the chemist says the youth can handle the next customer while he goes for a tea break, "And remember to put some poetry into it," he says.

Anyway, the youth waits, but nobody comes in, so after some time he decides to go to the toilet to relieve his bladder. Just then, a teenage girl comes in. "Can I help you?" he asks.

She replies very embarrassedly that she would like to buy some sanitary napkins, to which the youth replies poetically: "Hang on Miss, I'm dying for a piss, but I'll be back in a flash, with a sash for your gash!"

## The Laughing Customer

A man walks into a chemist store and asks for a pack of condoms. As soon as he has paid for them, he begins laughing and walks out.

The next day, the same performance, with the man walking out laughing as though his guts would spill out. The chemist finds this odd and tells his assistant that if the man returns, he should follow him.

Sure enough, he comes into the store on the third day, repeating his actions once more. The assistant duly follows the man.

Half an hour later, he returns. "So did you follow him to his hideout?"

"I did."

"And where did he go with the pack of condoms?"

"He went to your house...."

## Dead Man's Woe

A funeral procession was winding its way to the cemetery on top of the hill outside town, when the hearse hit a bump. The coffin was bumped loose, fell out onto the road and began sliding back towards town, as it was a steep hill. It slid faster and faster. Finally, it reached the town and was skidding its way down Main Street. Suddenly, at an intersection, the coffin hit a curb, flew onto the sidewalk, smashed through the front glass window of the chemist store, and slammed up against the prescription counter.

The lid popped off, the corpse sat up and asked: "You got anything to stop this damn coffin?"

## The Straight Duck

A duck walks into a chemist store and tells the chemist, "Give me a lipstick."

The chemist asks the duck, "Will that be cash or credit card?"

The duck replies, "Just put it on my bill."

The next day, the duck goes back to the chemist and tells the chemist, "Give me a box of condoms."

The chemist inquires, "Do you want me to also put them on your bill?"

The duck says, "Hell no! I'm not that kind of duck!"

## Advanced Pill

An advanced society has figured how to package basic knowledge in pill form. A student, needing some learning, goes to the chemist and inquires about what kind of knowledge pills are available.

The chemist says, "Here's a pill for English literature."

The student takes the pill and swallows it and has new knowledge about English literature! "What else do you have?" asks the student.

"Well, I have pills for art, biology, geography and history," replies the chemist.

The student asks for these, and swallows them and has new knowledge about those subjects. Then the student asks, "Do you have a pill for maths?"

The chemist says, "Just a moment," goes back into the storeroom, brings back a whopper of a pill, and plunks it on the counter.

"I have to take that huge pill for maths?" inquires the student.

The chemist replies, "Well, you know maths always was a little hard to swallow."

## Hand Practice

This guy goes to the chemist and says, "Listen, these two girls are coming to my place for the weekend and they are hot, very hot. Would you have something to get me going all night? It is going to be a hell of a party."

The chemist goes into the storeroom, comes back with an old dusty bottle and says, "This stuff is very potent, you drink only one ounce of it and I guarantee that you will be hard all night. Let me know about it."

The weekend goes by and on Monday morning, the chemist is going to work and at the door of the store, the same fellow is waiting for him. The chemist says, "What are you doing here so early? How was your weekend?"

The guy replies, "Quick open the store, I need Blue Ice (a muscle pain reliever)."

Knowing what the guy had been doing all weekend, the chemist says, "Are you crazy? You can't put that on your organ. The skin is way too sensitive."

The guy blurts out, "It's not for my organ, it's for my arm."

The chemist asks, "Why? What happened?"

The poor man replies, "Well... I drank the whole bottle of your potion."

Chemist: "And...."

"And the girls never turned up!" the guy moans.

## Memory Problems

A man walks into a chemist store and asks the chemist, "Do you have any acetylsalicylic acid?"

"You mean aspirin?" queries the chemist.

"That's it! I can never remember that word."

## Only This Much

A man walks into a chemist store and goes to the counter. Standing behind the counter is a young woman. "May I speak to the chemist?" he asks.

"Well," she replies, "I am the chemist!"

He looks very uncomfortable, and asks for a male chemist, as he has a "male problem". She informs him that only she and her sister work at this particular place. He blushes and says, "Well, I really do need help, so I guess I'll ask you... I have a problem. I have a constant erection, and nothing I do seems to get rid of it. It's been like this for three months now. Can you give me anything for it?"

The woman looks thoughtful, and says, "Hold on, I'll go inside and ask my sister."

After a couple of minutes she returns and says, "We'll give you 10,000 bucks, half of the business and the profits, but that's all we can give you for it..."

## Handy Job

A guy goes into a chemist store to buy condoms. The salesman asks, "What size?"

The guy says, "Gee, I don't know!"

The salesman says, "Go see Pinkie at Counter No. 4."

He goes over to see Pinkie; she grabs him in the crotch, and yells, "Medium!" The guy is mortified; he hurries over to pay and gets out of the store.

Another guy comes in to buy condoms, the salesman asks the size, and again sends him over to Pinkie at Counter No. 4. Pinkie grabs him and yells, "Large!" The guy struts over to the register, pays and leaves.

A high school kid comes in to buy condoms. The clerk says, "What size?"

The embarrassed kid says, "I've never done this before. I don't know what size."

The salesman sends him over to Pinkie at Counter No. 4. She grabs him and then yells, "Clean up at Counter No. 4! Clean up at Counter No. 4!"

## Cough, Cough...

Outside a chemist store in a busy street, a poor man is clutching onto a pole for dear life, not breathing, not moving, not twitching a muscle, just standing there, frozen. Seeing this strange sight in front of his store, the chemist goes up to his assistant and asks, "What's the matter with that guy? Wasn't he in here earlier?"

The assistant replies, "Yes, he was. He had the most terrible cough and none of my prescriptions seemed to help."

Chemist: "He seems to be fine now."

# Dental Drills

## Hold All

There's this call-girl who goes to the dentist. As he leans over to begin working on her, she grabs his balls. The dentist says, "Ma'am, I believe you've got hold of my privates."

The call-girl replies, "Oh yes. We're going to be careful not to hurt each other, aren't we?"

## Roll Call

What's worse than having your doctor tell you that you have VD?

Having your dentist tell you!

## Dental TM

Why did the two gurus refuse a painkiller when they went to the dentist?

One wanted to transcend dental medication.

The other wanted transcendental medication!

## Final Bargain

A dentist begs his patient: "Could you help me, please? Could you give out a few of your loudest, most painful screams?"

Patient: "But why? Doc, it isn't all that bad this time."

Dentist: "There are so many people in the waiting room right now and I don't want to miss the 8 o'clock one-day Champions Trophy final."

## Smart Alec

A smart alec dentist had a T-shirt which said on the front: Let me put my tool in your mouth...

And on the back: ...and I will fill your cavity.

## Slow Poke

Patient: "How much to have this tooth extracted?"

Dentist: "Only 500 bucks."

Patient: "What? You charge 500 bucks for just a few minutes' work!"

Dentist: "I can extract it very s-l-o-w-l-y if that's what you want."

## Slow Take

A dentist is getting ready to clean an elderly lady's teeth. He notices that she is a little nervous, so he begins to tell her a story as he is putting on his surgical gloves: "Do you know how they make these rubber gloves?"

"No?" she responds.

"Well," he bluffs, "down in Timbuktu they have this big building set up with a large tank of latex, and the workers are all picked according to hand size. Each individual walks up to the tank, dips their hands in, and then walks around for some time while the latex sets up and dries right onto their hands! Then they peel off the gloves and throw them into the big 'Finished Goods Crate' and start the process all over again."

Upon hearing this explanation the woman sits stoic, not laughing in the least.

A few minutes later, during the procedure, the dentist has to stop cleaning her teeth because she bursts out laughing. The dentist is baffled, and asks her what's so funny.

The woman blushes and exclaims, "I suddenly just thought about how they must make condoms!"

## Dental Break

A woman and her husband interrupt their vacation to go to the dentist. "I want a tooth pulled, and I don't want a painkiller because I'm in a big hurry," the woman says. "Just extract the tooth as quickly as possible, and we'll be on our way."

The dentist is quite impressed that she doesn't want a painkiller. "You're certainly a courageous woman," he says. "Which tooth is it?"

The woman turns to her husband and says: "Show him your tooth, darling."

## 18x54

A 54-year-old dentist ditches his wife of 30 years for an 18-year-old girl and writes his wife a note: "Sorry dear, but it's over between us, because I've found a sexy 18-year-old to spend the rest of my days with, having fun."

The wife sends him another note in response: "Thank you, dear! But I've also found an 18-year-old lover boy for myself to spend the rest of my life with, having fun. And let me tell you dear, that an 18-year-old lover boy goes many more times into a 54-year-old woman than a 54-year-old lover goes into an 18-year-old woman!"

# Multiple Practitioners' Shenanigans

## Daffy Definitions

How do you know which doctor is a urologist?

He is the one who washes his hands before he urinates.

Proctologist: A doctor who puts in a hard day at the orifice.

A proctologist is the rare profession in which the MD starts out at the bottom and stays there.

## Switch Over

A proctologist pulls out a thermometer from his shirt pocket. He looks at it and says, "Shit, some a***hole has my pen!"

## Pants Down

My husband is in danger of losing his licence to practise medicine. He was caught having sex with some of his patients. It's such a shame. He was the best mortician in town.

## Podiatric Cracks

- Did you hear about the two podiatrists who were archrivals?
- Podiatrists are good at thinking on your feet.
- Sign in podiatrist's office 'Toe Zone'.
- Podiatrists have a real foothold on the medical profession.

## Different Practitioners

There are several kinds of doctors, and it is said that they can be differentiated by the following method:

- General Practitioners know nothing and do little.
- Surgeons know little and do everything.
- Internists know everything and do nothing.
- Pathologists know everything and can do everything, but it's usually too late.

## Final Opening

A cardiac specialist died and at his funeral the coffin was placed in front of a huge mock-up of a heart made up of flowers. When the priest finished the sermon and eulogy, and after everyone had said their good-byes, the heart opened, the coffin rolled inside and the heart closed.

Just then one of the mourners burst into laughter. The guy next to him asked: "What's so funny?"

"I was thinking about my own funeral," the man replied.

"What's so funny about that?"

"I'm a gynaecologist," the man giggled.

## Acute Observation

A professor is giving the First Year medical students their first lecture on autopsies and decides to give them a few basics before starting. "You must be capable of two things to do an autopsy. The first thing is that you must have no sense of fear."

At this point, the lecturer sticks his finger into the dead man's anus and then licks it. He asks all the students to do the same thing with the corpses before them. After a couple of minutes' silence, they follow suit.

"The second thing is that you must have an acute sense of observation: I stuck my middle finger into the corpse's anus, but I licked my index finger!"

## Changing Tack

A medic arrives on the scene to find a paramedic performing CPR (cardiopulmonary resuscitation) with his hands over the woman's breast instead of over the sternum. The medic says, "Shouldn't you change your hand position?"

The paramedic says, "You're right!" So saying, he places his hands on the opposite breast!

## Name Game

Two doctors opened offices in a small town and put up a sign reading, "Dr Dave and Dr Datey, Psychiatry and Proctology."

The town fathers were not too happy with the sign, and proposed: "Hysteria and Posteriors."

The doctors didn't find it acceptable, so they suggested: "Schizoids and Haemorrhoids."

The town didn't like that either and countered with: "Catatonics and High Colonics."

Thumbs down again. By now the story was in the newspapers and suggestions began rolling in:

"Manic-depressives and Anal-retentive."

"Minds and Behinds."

"Lost Souls and A***holes."

"Analysis and Anal Cysts."

"Queers and Rears."

"Nuts and Butts."

"Freaks and Cheeks."

"Loons and Moons."

None of these satisfied one side or the other, but they finally settled on: "Dr Dave and Dr Datey, Odds and Ends."

## Feel-n-Tell

One night a man and a woman are both at a bar knocking back a few beers. They start talking and come to realise that they're both doctors. After about an hour, the man says to the woman, "Hey! How about sharing a bed together tonight? No strings attached. It'll just be one night of fun."

Randy as hell, the woman doctor agrees to it. So they go back to her place and he goes into the bedroom. She goes into the bathroom and starts scrubbing up like she's about to go into the operation theatre. She scrubs for a good 10 minutes.

Finally she goes into the bedroom and they have sex for an hour or so. Afterwards, the man says to the woman, "You're a surgeon, aren't you?"

"Yeah, how did you know?"

The man says, "I could tell by the way you scrubbed up before we started."

"Oh, that makes sense," says the woman. "You're an anaesthesiologist, aren't you?"

"Yeah," says the man, a bit surprised. "How did you know?"

"No problem," the woman answers. "Because I slept through most of it and didn't feel a thing!"

## Trick Treat

A doctor and a lawyer in two cars collided on a country road. The lawyer, seeing that the doctor was a little shaken up, helped him from the car and offered him a drink from his hip flask.

The doctor accepted, had a couple of pegs and handed the flask back to the lawyer, who closed it and put it away.

"Aren't you going to have a drink yourself?" asked the doctor.

"Sure, after the police leave!" replied the dirty attorney.

## Metered Calls

A doctor and a lawyer are talking at a party. Their conversation is constantly interrupted by people describing their ailments and asking the doctor for free medical advice…

After an hour of this, the exasperated doctor asks the lawyer: "What do you do to stop people from asking you for legal advice when you're out of the office?"

"I give it to them," replies the lawyer, "and then I send them a bill."

The doctor was shocked, but agrees to give it a try.

The next day, still feeling slightly guilty, the doctor prepares the bills. When he goes to post them, he glances at his mailbox and is dumbfounded – there's a bill for him from the lawyer!

## Strange Postcard

A doctor is having an affair with his nurse, and shortly after this begins, she announces that she is pregnant. Not wanting his wife to find out, he gives her a large amount of money and asks her to go out of the country, to Germany, to wait for the delivery and have the baby there.

"But how will you know when our baby is born?" she asks.

"Well," he says, "after you've had the baby, just send me a postcard and write 'sauerkraut' on the back."

Not knowing what else to do, she takes the money and goes off to Germany.

Six months go by until one day the doctor's wife calls him at his office. "Dear, there's a very strange postcard for you in the mail today," she explains. "I don't understand what it means!"

"Just wait till I get home and I'll read it," he replies.

Later that evening, the doctor comes home and reads his postcard, which says: "SAUERKRAUT, SAUERKRAUT, SAUERKRAUT – TWO WITH WIENERS, ONE WITHOUT!"

## Blind Shot

Three doctors are in a bird park and a bird flies overhead. The general practitioner looks at it and says, "Looks like a duck, flies like a duck... it's probably a duck," shoots at it but misses and the bird flies away.

The next bird flies overhead and the pathologist looks at it, then looks through the pages of a bird manual, and says, "Hmmmm... green wings, yellow bill, quacking sound... might be a duck." He raises his gun to shoot it, but the bird is gone by then.

A third bird flies over. The surgeon raises his gun and shoots almost without looking, brings the bird down, and turns to the pathologist and says, "Go see if that was a duck."

## Once or...

A doctor and a nurse have just got married. As they are lying in bed the second night, the doctor tells the nurse, "Honey, to avoid any problems, let's try the following system. When we go to bed at night, if you would like to have sex, pull my tool once...."

"And what if I don't want to have sex?" inquires the nurse.

"Oh, no probs!" says the doctor. "If you don't want to have sex, pull my tool 100 times!"

## Mute Un-mute

A mute man was walking down the street one day and chanced upon a friend of his (also a mute). In sign language, he inquired how his friend had been doing.

The friend replied (vocally!), "Oh, can that hand-waving crap. I can talk now."

Intrigued, the mute pressed him for details. It seems that he had gone to a specialist, who, seeing no physical damage, had put him on a treatment programme that had restored the use of his vocal chords. Gesturing wildly, the mute asked if he might meet this specialist.

They got an appointment that very afternoon.

After an exam, the specialist proclaims that there was no permanent damage, that the mute was essentially in the same condition as his buddy and that there is no reason why he couldn't be helped as well.

"Yes, yes," signs the mute. "Let's have the first treatment right now!"

"Very well," replies the specialist. "Kindly go into the next room, drop your pants and lean over the examining table. I'll be right in."

The mute does as instructed and the doctor sneaks in with a broomstick, hammer and jar of Vaseline. Greasing the broom handle, he "sends it home" with a few deft swipes of the hammer. The mute jumps from the table, screaming, "AAAAAAAAaaaaaaaaaa!!!"

"Very good," smiles the doctor. "Next Tuesday, we start with 'B'."

## Sign Problems

Doctors at a hospital in Mumbai have gone on strike. Hospital officials say they will find out what the doctors' demands are as soon as they can get a chemist over there to read the picket signs!

# The Surgeon's Special

## Polish Cracks

One Polish surgeon asks another: "How did that appendectomy go?"

"Appendectomy?" shrieks the other. "I thought it was an autopsy!"

*Was that smaller breasts and a larger nose or the other way around?*

## Screwed Right

A well-known rich businessman's wife broke her hip. The businessman got the best bone surgeon in town to do the operation. The operation consisted of lining up the broken hip and putting in a screw to secure it. The operation went off smoothly and the surgeon sent the businessman a bill of Rs 50,000 for his services.

The businessman was outraged at the cost and sent the doctor a letter demanding an itemised list of the costs.

The doctor sent back a list with two things:

1 screw Re 1 only

Knowing how to put it in the right place

Rs 49,999 = Rs 50,000 total.

The businessman paid up without further argument.

## Navel Specialist

"What kind of job do you do?" a lady passenger asked the man travelling in the first-class compartment.

"I'm a naval surgeon," he replied.

"Goodness! A navel surgeon!" exclaimed the lady. "How you doctors specialise these days!"

## Hard Rolls

A man goes to a doctor to have his tool enlarged. However, this particular procedure involves suturing a baby elephant's trunk onto the man's organ. Overjoyed, the man goes out with his girlfriend to a very fancy restaurant. After cocktails, the man's tool creeps out of his pants, feels around the table, grabs a hard roll and quickly disappears under the tablecloth.

The girl is startled and exclaims, "What was that?"

Suddenly, the tool comes back, takes another hard roll and just as quickly disappears. The girl is silent for a moment, then finally says, "I don't believe I saw what I think I just saw... Can you do that again?"

With a weak smile, the man replies, "Honey, I'd like to, but I don't think my butt can take another hard roll!"

## Hole Model

An American, an Englishman and a Japanese fellow were discussing their respective countries over drink at a London pub one evening. The English fellow mentioned how British medicine had progressed so far that doctors recently had taken a single liver, cut it into six pieces, then transplanted it into six separate men in need of a healthy liver. This had resulted in six new workers in the job market.

At this, the Japanese guy said that in his country doctors had cut a lung into twelve pieces, transplanted these into 12 people in need of healthy lungs, thereby putting 12 new people in the job market.

Not to be outdone, the American said, "That's nothing. In the US, we took one a***hole, made it President, and now there are 10 million people in the market looking for a job!"

## Inveterate Coffee Pot

There was this guy in hospital scheduled for surgery. On the morning of his operation, he starts yelling that he wants coffee. The nurse asks him to be quiet, as he is disturbing the other patients.

"But I've had coffee every morning for 40 years and I want a cup of coffee NOW!" he screams.

The nurse replies, "Now sir, you realise that you are due to go into surgery in an hour and you can't have anything in your stomach. Couldn't you do without coffee just this once?"

The guy rants and raves even more and the doctor comes in to see what the racket is all about. The nurse explains the situation and the doctor turns to the belligerent man, "You understand that you can't have anything in your stomach before the surgery, don't you?"

"I don't care. I want some coffee. NOW!"

The doctor thinks for a minute and says, "Very well. The only way we can give you any coffee is through an enema. Is that good enough?"

The guy pauses and replies, "Well, if that's the only way I can get some coffee around in this damn joint..."

So the doctor tells the nurse to give him a coffee enema to keep him quiet. The nurse returns with an enema bag and a fresh pot of hot coffee. She pours it into the bag, greases up the applicator and sticks it up the guy's butt.

"Ahhh! Hot coffee!" the guy says in a satisfied tone.

Then, a few seconds later, he suddenly starts bitching and complaining again. "What's the matter this time?" the exasperated nurse yells.

"The coffee's too sweet!" the guy scowls.

## Hole-n-Sole

Once when I was sick to the gills, I went to a ear, nose and throat specialist to get well. Now, come to think of it, there are ear doctors, nose doctors, throat doctors, gynaecologists, proctologists – any damn place you got a hole, there's a doctor who specialises in your hole! They make an entire career out of that particular hole.

And if the ear doctor, nose doctor, throat doctor, gynaecologist or proctologist can't help you, he sends you to a surgeon. Why?

So he can make a new hole!

## Hard Times

While doing a vasectomy, the doctor slipped and cut off one of the man's balls. To avoid a huge malpractice suit, he decides to replace the missing ball with an onion. Several weeks later, the patient returns for a check-up.

"How's your sex life?" the doctor asks.

"Pretty good," the man says, much to the doctor's relief. But then he adds, "I've had some strange side effects."

"What's that?" the doctor asks anxiously.

"Well, every time I piss, my eyes water. When my wife gives me a blowjob, she gets heartburn. And every time I pass an onion pakora vendor, I get a hard-on."

## Heart Find

A new arrival, about to enter the hospital, saw two white-coated doctors searching through the flowerbeds. "Excuse me," he inquires, "have you lost something?"

"No," replies one of the doctors. "We're doing a heart transplant for an income-tax officer and want to find a suitable stone."

## Wrong Chop

A man goes to his surgeon and says, "I want to be castrated."

"What?" says the doctor, "surely you don't want that."

"Yes," says the man, "that's what I want. In fact, I insist."

So the doctor told him to check into the hospital. When he did, he was stripped, laid on a stretcher, wheeled into the operation theatre, anaesthetised, and CHOP! – off went his testicles.

The next day, he wakes up in a double room and, wanting to be sociable, asks the man in the next bed what he is in for.

"Oh, I was circumcised," the man says.

"Son of a gun! That's the word I was looking for!" blurts out the castrated man.

## Size Wise

A really handsome man had a high squeaky voice. He was always surrounded by girls; the only problem was that they ran off the moment he opened his mouth and they heard his voice. So he went to the ENT surgeon.

The surgeon said he could fix the problem by cutting off the man's tool. The man agreed to the surgery, and sure enough his voice returned to normal and he was surrounded by women once again. And now they didn't run off on hearing him.

Later, the man decided to get a whole new wardrobe. The tailor took a look at him and rattled of figures ending up with underwear size 36.

The man said: "No, I wear size 30."

And the tailor replied, "I've been doing this for years – trust me. If you wore size 30, your voice would be high and squeaky."

## Squeak, Squeak

And there's this other man who went to see the same ENT surgeon because of a very high, squeaky, annoying voice. The surgeon examined him and told him that the only way out would be to replace his extremely large organ with a smaller one. The guy is desperate and decides to undergo the operation. It's a great success and the man acquires a fantastic baritone.

But after some time the guy's sex life deteriorates and he decides to see the doctor to try and get his original equipment back.

He tells the surgeon, "Doctor, is there any way that you could get me my organ back? My sex life has gone to the dogs."

"Not on your life! I can't," the surgeon replies in a very high, squeaky, annoying voice.

## Dick Trick

A man goes to have plastic surgery on his injured tool. The doctor examines him and asks, "How did this happen?"

"Well, doc, I stay in a locality where people live in mobile vans," the man explains. "And from where I am, I can see this absolutely stunning and gorgeous babe. She's luscious and built like an hourglass – all curves. Anyway, she's so horny that every night I see her take a hotdog from the refrigerator and stick it in a hole in the floorboard of her mobile van. Then she gets down and pleasures herself on the hotdog."

"And?" the doctor asks with rising anticipation.

"Well," says the man, "I felt that this was a lot of wasted pussy. So, one day, I slid myself underneath her trailer and when she put the hotdog into the hole, I removed it and substituted my dick. It was a great idea and everything was going real good, too. Then someone knocked at her door, and she jumped off my hotdog and tried to kick it under the sofa!"

## Depreciated Value

The relatives gathered in the hospital waiting room, where their family member lay gravely ill. Finally, the surgeon came in looking tired and sombre. "I'm afraid I have some bad news," he said as he surveyed the worried faces. "The only hope left for your loved one at this time is a brain transplant. It's an experimental procedure, semi-risky, and you will have to pay for the brain yourselves."

The family members were silent as they absorbed the news. After some time, someone asked, "How much does a brain cost?"

The doctor quickly responded, "Rs 100,000 for a male brain, and Rs 10,000 for a female brain."

The moment turned awkward. Men in the room tried not to smile, avoiding eye contact with the women, but some actually smirked. A man, unable to control his curiosity, blurted out the question everyone wanted to ask, "Why is the male brain much more expensive?"

The doctor smiled at the childish question and said, "It's just standard pricing procedure. We have to mark down the price of the female brains because they've been used!"

## Surgeon's Choice

Four surgeons are taking a coffee break and discussing their work. The first surgeon says, "I think accountants are the easiest to operate on. You open them up and everything inside is numbered."

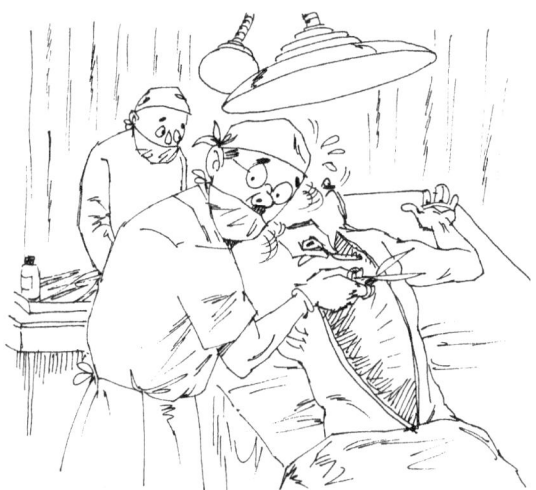

The second surgeon responds, "I think librarians are the easiest to operate on. You open them up and everything is in alphabetical order."

The third surgeon rebuts, "I think electricians are the easiest to operate on. You open them up and everything is colour-coded."

The fourth surgeon closes the argument, "I think lawyers are the easiest to operate on. They're heartless, spineless, gutless, and their heads and butt are interchangeable."

## The Three Bouquets

Liz Taylor goes in to see her cosmetic surgeon. "I have met the man of my dreams, finally!" she announces. "But I need you to help me with a small problem. This man is only 18 years old. I am truly head over heels in love with him, and don't want to disappoint him in any way, so I want you to make my private part look like that of an 18-year-old."

The surgeon agrees to perform the operation. "But one thing," Liz says, "you have to swear no one will know about this operation and no magazines or tabloids hear about it!"

"I swear Liz," the surgeon replies.

The big day arrives, Liz is anaesthetised, the operation goes off perfectly and she is moved to a recovery room. Upon regaining consciousness, Liz's eyes focus on three huge bouquets at the foot of her bed. As the surgeon enters the room to check on her, Liz bursts into tears.

"How could you do this to me? You swore that not a soul would hear of this operation!" cries Liz, pointing accusingly at the three bouquets.

"Now, now Liz! I didn't tell a soul. The first bouquet is from me. I've been your friend, as much as your surgeon, for the past 10 years. I just wanted to make you feel good. The second one is from the anaesthesiologist; he's gay, he's one of your biggest fans, and I thought it was okay, since he worked side by side with me on your operation."

Liz's eyes gazed at the third bouquet. "And who sent those?"

"Oh those!" the surgeon replies. "Those are from the guy in the burns unit, who wanted to thank you for his new ears!"

## Pricey Brains

A guy goes to a brain surgeon to have a transplant. He says, "OK doc, what do you have?"

The doctor says, "Well there's a physician's brain, that's Rs 10,000 an ounce."

"OK, what else?"

"Well, there's a politician's brain, that's Rs 100,000 an ounce."

The patient scratches his head and says, "I can see why it's that pricey for a physician's brain, but why is it so expensive for a politician's brain?"

"Do you know how many politicians it takes to make an ounce of brains?"

## Oral Science

A surgeon came to see his pop star patient on the morning after her operation. The young woman asked him, somewhat hesitantly, how long it would be before she could resume her normal sex life.

"I really haven't thought about it," gulped the stunned surgeon. "You're the first patient who's asked me that question after a tonsillectomy!"

## Chintu and Buddhu

Buddhu and Chintu were out cutting wood when Chintu cut his arm off accidentally. Buddhu remained calm, wrapped the arm in a plastic bag, and took the arm and Chintu to a surgeon.

"You are in luck," said the surgeon. "I am an expert in re-attaching limbs. Come back in four hours when I have completed the operation."

So Buddhu returned in four hours and the surgeon said, "I did it faster than I expected. Chintu is down at the pub." Buddhu rushed down to the pub and was amazed to see Chintu downing a peg.

A few weeks later, Buddhu and Chintu were cutting wood again when Chintu accidentally cut off his leg. Buddhu put the leg in a plastic bag and took the leg and Chintu back to the same surgeon.

"Legs are harder," said the surgeon, "but I'll see what I can do — come back in six hours."

Buddhu returned in six hours and the surgeon said, "I finished early — Chintu's playing football." Buddhu went to the ground and was surprised to find Chintu kicking 50-metre torpedoes.

A few weeks later, Buddhu and Chintu were cutting wood again, when Chintu accidentally cut off his own head. Buddhu put the head in a plastic bag and took the head and the rest of Chintu to the surgeon, confident that the skilful surgeon would do the job.

"Gosh, heads are really difficult to re-attach," the surgeon muttered, "but I'll see what I can do — come back in 12 hours."

Buddhu returned in 12 hours. "How did it go, doc?" he asked.

"I'm sorry, Chintu's dead," the surgeon said. "He suffocated in the plastic bag, you stupid fool!"

## 10 things you dread hearing during surgery:

1. Better save that. We'll need it for the autopsy.
2. That was some party last night. I can't remember when I've been that drunk.
3. Wait a minute! If this is his spleen, what's that?
4. OOPS! Say, has anyone ever survived 500 ML of this stuff before?
5. Damn it! There goes the power again.
6. You know, there's big money in kidneys. Hey, guess what, this guy's got two!
7. Could you stop that thing from beating? It's distracting me!
8. OK, now take a picture from this angle. This is truly a freak of nature.
9. What do you mean he wasn't in for a sex change!
10. Damn! Page 47 of the operation manual is missing!

# Psychiatric Feedback

## Gentle Therapist

The psychotherapist, Dr Nari Vaswani, was in the dock for assaulting the signboard painter and everyone was baffled as to why a gentle man like him had assaulted somebody, a poor signboard painter at that.

The defence attorney sought to convince the judge that the assault was not premeditated and had been provoked by the illiterate painter's sheer incompetence. The judge seemed unmoved. To convince His Lordship, the defence attorney then held up the offending signboard. It read:

<u>Dr Nari Vaswani</u>

Psycho the rapist

The psychotherapist was immediately acquitted!

☺   ❖   ☺

## Guess What...

Why do psychiatrists give their patients shock treatment?

To prepare them for the bill!

☺   ❖   ☺

## Double Takes

Patient: "Doctor, I have a split personality."

Psychiatrist: "Nurse, bring in another chair."

☺   ❖   ☺

"I'm treating a patient with a split personality," boasted a psychiatrist, "and Mediclaim pays for both of them!"

A psychiatrist, who was just starting out, advertised his clinic as follows: "Satisfaction guaranteed or your mania back."

Sign on a psychologist's office: Schizophrenics pay double.

Patient (suffering from inferiority and superiority complex) to psychiatrist: "I can't help it, doctor. I keep thinking that my inferiority complex is bigger and better than anyone else's!"

Anyone who goes to a psychiatrist ought to have his head examined!

What is the best thing about schizophrenia? You're never alone!

What is the worst thing about schizophrenia? Paying more than once for everything.

The two psychiatrists have just finished having sex and the first one turns to the other and says, "It was good for you, was it good for me?"

I had to kill my psychiatrist. He helped me a lot, but he knew too much.

How do you tell the difference between the psychiatrists and patients at the mental hospital?

The patients are the ones that eventually get better and go home!

## Tale of Depression

At the psychiatrist's office a homely woman came in depressed. "I'm lonely. I have no friends. Doctor, can you help me accept my ugliness?"

Psychiatrist: "I think I can. Go lie face down on the couch."

## Egg-n-Chicken Syndrome

Psychiatrist: "What's wrong with your brother?"

Girl: "He thinks he's a hen."

Psychiatrist: "How long has he been acting like a hen?"

Girl: "Three years. We would have come in sooner, but we needed the eggs."

## The Horse Syndrome

Wife: "Doctor, my husband thinks he's a horse."

Psychiatrist: "He is just probably a little stressed out and needs some rest."

Wife: "But he kicks chairs and eats grass and does not even sleep in the bed."

Psychiatrist: "Well, in that case, it looks like he may need a lot of help. But it may cost quite a lot of money for prolonged treatment."

Wife: "Oh, you don't have to worry about the money part. Last Sunday, my husband won the Pune horse derby!"

☺ ❖ ☺

## Card Syndrome

Patient: "Doctor, I keep thinking I'm a deck of cards!"

Psychiatrist: "Sit over there and I'll deal with you later."

☺ ❖ ☺

## Bridge Syndrome

Patient: "Doctor, I feel like a bridge..."

Psychiatrist: "What's come over you?"

Patient: "Two trucks, five cars, three tempos..."

☺ ❖ ☺

## Assorted Syndromes

Patient: "Doctor, I keep thinking I'm a dustbin!"

Psychiatrist: "Don't talk such rubbish!"

☺ ❖ ☺

Patient: "Doctor, people tell me I'm a wheelbarrow."

Psychiatrist: "Don't let people push you around."

☺ ❖ ☺

Patient: "Doctor, I keep thinking I'm a curtain."

Psychiatrist: "Pull yourself together!"

☺ ❖ ☺

Patient: "Doctor, my wife thinks I'm crazy because I like sausages."

Psychiatrist: "Nonsense! I like sausages too."

Patient: "Good, you should come and see my collection. I've got hundreds of them at home!"

Patient: "Doctor, my husband thinks I'm crazy because I love sausages."

Psychiatrist: "Nothing wrong with that. I'm also fond of sausages."

Patient: "Sexy beasts, aren't they?"

You have to admit we would be a well-matched couple!

## Dirty Pictures

A patient goes to a psychiatrist. The psychiatrist gives him a Rorschach Test. He shows the patient a circle with a dot inside it and asks, "What do you see?"

Patient: "Two people are having sex in the middle of a circular room."

The psychiatrist shows the patient another picture of a square with a dot inside it and asks, "What do you see?"

Patient: "Two people are having sex in a square room."

The psychiatrist shows the patient one more picture of a triangle with a dot inside it: "What do you see now?"

Patient: "Doctor, are you some kind of pervert?"

Another patient goes to see the same psychiatrist, who gives this patient also a Rorschach Test. On seeing a circle with a dot inside it, the patient says, "A couple are having sex inside a circular room."

Ditto with the square with a dot inside and a triangle with a dot inside. Exasperated, the psychiatrist asks, "Is sex all you can see and think about?"

"Hey!" responds the indignant patient. "Who's been showing me all those dirty pictures?"

☺ ❖ ☺

## Fridge Fare

Man: "Doctor, my wife thinks she's a refrigerator!"

Psychiatrist: "Don't worry! It will pass."

Man: "But, doctor, when she sleeps with her mouth open, the damn refrigerator light disturbs me!"

☺ ❖ ☺

## Shy No More

Hypnotist: "Okay, Mr Wandrewala, when I say 'wake up', you will no longer be shy but full of confidence and be able to speak your mind… Wake up!"

Patient: "Right, you! How about giving me a refund, you money-grabbing old hypnotic fake!"

☺ ❖ ☺

## Fun in Absence

A psychiatrist on his rounds in a mental hospital sees a couple of patients behaving rather strangely. The first man is sitting on the edge of his bed clutching an imaginary steering wheel and making loud train noises: "Cooo-Cooo… Whoooo-Whooooo…"

"What are you doing?" enquires the doctor.

"I'm taking a train to Amritsar," replies the man.

Somewhat taken aback but not to be put off, the doctor moves on to the next bed where he can see some very energetic activity going on underneath the covers. On pulling them back he finds a man totally naked face down into the mattress. "And what are you doing?" asks the doctor, a little perplexed.

"Well," pants the man, "while he's away in Amritsar, I'm having it out with his wife!"

## The Beaten Path
Be a better psychiatrist and the world will beat a psychopath to your door.

## Right Match
A man walked into a psychiatrist's office, sat down and took out a pack of cigarettes. He removed a cigarette from the pack, unrolled it and stuffed the tobacco up his nose. The shrink frowned and said, "I see you need my help!"

The guy said, "Yeah, doc. Got a match?!"

## Troubled Brother

A man walks into the psychiatrist's office with a parantha on his head, half-fried eggs on each shoulder, and a strip of bacon over each ear. Humouring him, the shrink asks, "What seems to be the problem?"

The guy answers, "Doc, I'm worried about my brother."

## Hey Rama!

A man who thought he was Hanuman was disturbing the neighbourhood, so for public safety, he was committed to the Pune Mental Asylum. He was put in a room with another nut case and immediately began his routine, "I am Hanuman! Lord Rama has sent me!"

The other guy looks at him and declares, "I did NOT!"

## Reverse Cure

A man walks into a bar and orders a beer. He drinks the beer, then stands on the bar, drops his pants and pisses all over the place. The bartender freaks out. "You dirty pig! How dare you come into my bar and urinate! I'll beat the shit out of you..."

The man begins crying. "I'm sorry! It's ruining my life. I can't sleep. I do it every time I have a drink! It's worrying me to death, please don't hit me..."

The bartender feels sorry for the bloke. "Look, I have a brother who is a psychiatrist; here's his card, why don't you see him?"

The man hugs the bartender, shakes his hand and leaves with a thousand thanks...

Six months later, the man walks into the bar, and orders a drink. The bartender says, "Okay, here you go... Wait! Weren't you that guy who...?"

"Yes, and I went and saw your brother. He is fantastic. I am completely cured," chirps the man.

"Well, that's great. This beer is on the house," gushes the bartender.

So the man drinks the beer, stands on the bar, drops his trousers and pisses all over. "You bastard! I thought you said you were cured!" the bartender howls.

"I am! It doesn't bother me anymore!"

## Paper Talk

The head doctors in a lunatic asylum had a meeting and decided that one of their patients was potentially well. So they decide to test him and take him to the movies. When they get to the movie theatre, there are signs of wet paint pointing to the benches. The doctors just sit down, but the patient puts a newspaper down first and then sits down. The doctors get all excited because they think maybe he's in touch with reality now.

So they ask him, "Why did you put the newspaper down first?"

He answers, "Simple. So I'd be higher and get a better view!"

## Tight Talk

"Oh doctor!" moans the woman to the psychiatrist. "I don't know why everyone calls me a nymphomaniac."

"I understand," says the shrink. "But I'll be able to take better notes if you'll let go of my cock."

## The Long-n-Short of...

A psychiatrist visited the Pune Mental Asylum and asked a patient, "How did you get here?"

"Well," the man drawled, "it all started when I got married and I guess I should never have done it. I got hitched to a widow with a grown daughter who then became my stepdaughter. My daddy came to visit us, fell in love with my lovely stepdaughter, and then married her. And so my stepdaughter was now my stepmother.

"Soon, my wife had a son who was, of course, my daddy's brother-in-law since he is the half-brother of my stepdaughter, who is now, of course, my daddy's wife. So, as I told you, when my stepdaughter married my daddy, she was at once my stepmother! Now, since my new son is brother to my stepmother, he also became my uncle. As you know, my wife is my step-grandmother since she is my stepmother's mother. Don't forget that my stepmother is my stepdaughter. Remember, too, that I am my wife's grandson.

"But hold on just a few moments more. You see, since I'm married to my step-grandmother, I am not only the wife's grandson and her hubby, but I am also my own grandfather. Now can you understand how I got put in this asylum?"

## Passing Thoughts

Two psychiatrists pass each other in the hall. The first says, "Hello!"

The other gets thinking, "I wonder what he meant by that?"

## Repeat Problem

A research group advertised for participants in a study of obsessive-compulsive disorder. They were looking for therapy clients who had been diagnosed with this disorder. The response was gratifying; they got 3,000 responses about three days after the ad came out.

All from the same person!

## Problem Solved

A young woman goes to a psychiatrist. When she walked into his office, he said, "Take off your clothes and get on the couch."

A little confused, she did as he asked. He took off his pants and had sex with her on the couch.

When he finished, he said, "Well, my problem is solved. Now, what's yours?"

## Looney Talk

A man who thinks he's Shivaji Maharaj has been seeing a psychiatrist. He finishes one session by telling the doctor, "Tomorrow, we'll cross the Deccan and surprise the Mughals when they least expect it."

As soon as he's gone, the psychiatrist picks up the phone and says, "Aurangzeb, this is Afzal Khan. I have the Marathas' plans!"

☺  ❖  ☺

## Big Boob Fixation

The other day, while I was seeing my shrink, he asked me what I looked for in a woman. Naturally, I replied, "Big boobs!"

He said, "No, I meant for a serious relationship."

So I said, "Oh, seriously – big boobs!"

"No, no, no," he remonstrated. "I mean what do you look for in the one woman you want to spend the rest of your life with?"

He looked at me kind of worried as I just sat there on his couch laughing until my gut hurt. "Spend the rest of my life with one woman? No woman's boobs are THAT big!"

## Psychiatric Hotline

Recording: Hello! Welcome to the Psychiatric Hotline!

- ✦ If you are Obsessive-Compulsive, please press 1, repeatedly.
- ✦ If you are co-dependent, please ask someone to press 2.
- ✦ If you have multiple personalities, please press 3, 4, 5 and 6.
- ✦ If you are paranoid-delusional, we KNOW who you are and what you want. Just stay on the line until we trace the call.
- ✦ If you are schizophrenic, listen carefully and a little voice will tell you what to do next.
- ✦ If you are manic-depressive, it doesn't matter which number you press. No one will answer.
- ✦ If you are paranoid, the thing you are holding to your ear is loaded and ready to blow up.
- ✦ If you are Oedipal, your mother would like to speak with you — please stay on the line.

## Loose Talk

A guy had been feeling down for so long that he finally decided to seek the aid of a psychiatrist. He went there, lay on the couch, spilled his guts out, then waited for the profound wisdom of the psychiatrist to make him feel better.

The psychiatrist asked a few questions, took some notes, then sat thinking in silence for a few minutes with a puzzled look on his face.

Suddenly, he looked up with an expression of delight and said, "Um, I think your problem is low self-esteem. It is very common among losers like you!"

## Over and Under

Shankar went to a psychiatrist. "Doc," he said, "I've got trouble. Every time I get into bed, I think there's somebody under it. I get under the bed, I think there's somebody on top of it. Top, under, top, under... You got to help me, I'm going crazy!"

"Just put yourself in my hands for two years," said the doctor. "Come to me thrice a week and I'll cure your fears."

"How much do you charge?"

"Two thousand bucks per visit."

"Two thousand bucks! Let me sleep over it!" said Shankar.

Six months later, the doctor met Shankar on the street. "Why didn't you come to see me again?" asked the psychiatrist.

"For two thousand bucks per visit? A bartender cured me for ten bucks."

"Is that so! How?"

"Simple. He told me to cut the legs of the bed!"

# Gynaecological Openings

## Live Check-up

The young lady entered the doctor's office carrying an infant. "Doctor," she explained, "the baby seems to be ailing. Instead of gaining weight, he lost three ounces this week."

The medic examined the child and then started to squeeze the girl's breasts. He unbuttoned her blouse, removed the bra and began sucking powerfully on one nipple.

"Young lady," he finally announced, "no wonder the baby is losing weight – you haven't any milk!"

"Of course not!" she shrieked. "It's not my child, it's my sister's!"

## Polish Wisdom

A Polish woman went to a gynaecologist and complained: "Doctor, when I wasn't married, I had six abortions, and now I am married and can't get pregnant."

"Evidently you don't breed in captivity," the gynaecologist noted.

A Polish woman goes to a gynaecologist for a check-up. She seems to be very embarrassed and uncomfortable. "Haven't you been examined like this before?" asks the doctor.

"Many times," she giggles, "but never by a doctor."

Another Polish woman visits a gynaecologist for an examination. He tells her to undress and lie down.

She asks: "But will you marry me?"

Problems with fertility drugs.

## Openings Galore

A young doctor just out of medical school announced to his girlfriend that he planned to specialise in gynaecology. When she asked him why he chose gynaecology, he smiled, "Aha! There are lots of openings!"

## Complimentary Take

The randy young gynaecologist took one look at his voluptuous new patient and abandoned his professional ethics entirely. As he stroked the supple skin of her naked body, he asked, "Do you understand what I am doing?"

"Yes," the patient answered. "You're checking for dermatological abrasions."

"Correct," the doctor lied.

Next, he fondled her breasts lovingly. Again, he inquired, "Do you understand what I am doing?"

"You're feeling for cancerous lumps," she ventured.

"Very astute," the doctor complimented, getting more excited. He placed the woman's feet in stirrups, dropped his pants, and slipped his member inside her. "And do you understand what I am doing now?"

"All too well," the patient shot back. "You're now contracting herpes and AIDS!"

## Daffynitions

What is the difference between a genealogist and a gynaecologist?

One looks up the family tree and the other looks up the family bush!

## Come Again…

Did you hear about the Sikh gynaecologist who used both hands? He wanted a second opinion.

## Free Private Shake

One woman says to another, "I can't understand why you haven't gone to see that new gynaecologist yet! I mean he's so young and handsome! And your gynaecologist is so old!"

The other woman replies with a smile, "Yeah, I know. But my gynaec's hands shake all the time!"

## Hotline Stuff

After much soul searching and having determined that the husband was infertile, the childless couple decided to try artificial insemination. When the woman showed up at the clinic, she was told to undress from the waist down, get on the table and place her feet in the stirrups. She was feeling rather awkward about the entire procedure when the doctor came in. Her anxiety was not diminished by the sight of him pulling down his pants!

"Wait a minute! What the hell is going on here?" yelped the woman, pulling herself into a sitting position.

"Don't you want to get pregnant?" asked the doctor.

"Well, yes, I do," answered the woman.

"Then lie back and spread 'em," replied the doctor. "We're all out of the bottled stuff. You'll just have to settle for what's on tap!"

## Tight Openings

There was a gynaecologist who was just SICK of his job. He wanted to do something else, so he decided to go back to school to be a mechanic. After six weeks, the final exam rolled around. When the instructor handed him his test, he noticed that he had received 200% marks. Curious as to how this was possible, he hung back after class to talk to the instructor.

"Sir, I noticed that I got 200% on my test. How come?"

"Well, I gave you 50% for dismantling the engine completely and properly. I gave you an additional 50% for reconstructing the engine completely and properly. And I gave you the final 100% for doing it all through the tailpipe!"

## Changing Times

A middle-aged woman seemed afraid and embarrassed as she visited her gynaecologist on an emergency call. "Come now," coaxed the doctor, "you've been seeing me for years! There's nothing you can't tell me."

"But this is kind of strange..." said the woman.

"Let me be the judge of that," the doctor replied.

"Well," said the woman, "yesterday I went to the bathroom in the morning and I heard a plink-plink in the toilet. When I looked down, the water was full of coins."

"Mmmm, I see," said the doctor.

"And that afternoon I went again and there were 50-paise coins in the bowl!"

"Uh-huh!" the doctor said, as he got more and more interested in her story.

"That night, there were 50-paise coins and this morning there were 25-paise coins! You've got to tell me what's wrong with me!" she implored. "I'm scared out of my wits!"

The gynaecologist put a comforting hand on her shoulder. "There, there. It's nothing to be frightened about," he said. "You're simply going through the change!"

# Obstetrician's Day

## Number 96 and...

A young father-to-be, Mansukh Rathod was waiting anxiously outside the Lamba Maternity Home ward where his wife was giving birth to their first baby. As he paced the floor, a nurse popped her head around the door. "It's a boy, Mr Rathod," she said. "But we think you'd better go and have a cup of coffee because there might be another!"

Mansukh turned a little pale and left. Some time later, he rang the hospital and was told he was the father of twins. "But," the nurse went on, "we're sure there's another on the way. Ring back again in a little while."

At that, Mansukh decided that coffee was not nearly strong enough. He ordered a few beers and rang the hospital again, only to be told a third baby had arrived and a fourth was imminent. White-faced, he stumbled to the bar and ordered a double scotch. Twenty minutes later, he tried the phone again, but he was in such a state that he dialled the wrong number and got the recorded cricket score.

When they picked him up — unconscious — off the floor of the phone booth, the recording was still going strong, "The score is 96 for nine and the last one was a duck!"

## Pain Talk

A woman goes to her doctor who verifies that she is pregnant. This is her first pregnancy. The doctor asks her if she has any questions. She replies, "Well, I'm a little worried about the pain. How much will childbirth hurt?"

The doctor answers, "Well, that varies from woman to woman and pregnancy to pregnancy and besides, it's difficult to describe pain."

"I know, but can't you give me some idea?" she asks.

"Grab your upper lip and pull it out a little..."

"Like this?"

"A little more..."

"Like this?"

"No. A little more..."

"Like this?"

"Yes. Does that hurt?"

"A little bit."

"Now stretch it over your head!"

## The First or...

A man speaks frantically into the phone, "My wife is pregnant and her contractions are only two minutes apart!"

"Is this her first child?" the doctor queries.

"No, you idiot!" the man shouts. "This is her husband!"

## Number Game

I was sitting in the waiting room of the hospital after my wife had gone into labour and the nurse walked out and said to the man sitting next to me, "Congratulations sir, you're the father of twins!"

The man replied, "How about that, I work for the Doublemint Chewing Gum Company." The man then followed the nurse to his wife's room.

About an hour later, the same nurse entered the waiting room and announced that Mr Tripathi's wife had just delivered triplets. Tripathi stood up and said, "Well, how do you like that, I work for the 3-D Company."

The gentleman sitting next to me then got up and started to leave. When I asked him why he was leaving, he remarked, "I think I need a breath of fresh air." Pausing, the man continued, "I work for 7-Up."

## Fine Print

A young woman, two months pregnant, went to see her obstetrician. He was in a hurry to leave on an emergency call, so he asked her to quickly bare her stomach, then reached into his desk and took out a rubber stamp, which he pressed beside her navel. He then rushed off.

At home, she and her husband tried to read the tiny words printed on her belly, but they were too small. They then found a magnifying glass and tried to read the words; the stamp read: "When your husband can read this without his glasses, it's time to get yourself to the hospital."

## Light Woes

Sukh Ram's wife went into labour in the middle of the night at their remote village and the government doctor was called to assist in the delivery. To keep the father-to-be busy, the doctor handed him a lantern and said: "Here, you hold this high so I can see what I'm doing."

Soon, a lusty baby boy was brought into the world. "Ouch!" said the doctor. "Don't be in a rush to put the lantern down... I think there's yet another little one coming along."

Sure enough, within minutes he had delivered a bonnie girl. "No, don't be in a great hurry to put down that lantern, young man... It seems there's yet another one besides!" cried the doctor.

Sukh Ram scratched his head in bewilderment and asked the doctor: "Doctor, by any chance, do you suppose the light's attracting them?"

## Creepy Crawly

The old government doctor went out to the remote village to deliver a baby. It was so far out, there was no electricity. When the doctor arrived, no one was home except for the labouring mother and her 3-year-old son. The doctor instructed the child to hold a lantern high so he could see while he helped the woman deliver the baby. The boy did so, the mother pushed and, after a little while, the doctor lifted the newborn by the feet and spanked him on the bottom to get him to take his first breath....

"Hit him again," the 3-year-old yelled. "He shouldn't have crawled up there in the first place!"

## Multi-sexual

A lady in New York in the delivery room was starting to deliver her baby. As it made its appearance it was dark and had curly hair. The doctor said, "Ma'am, have you ever slept with a black man?"

She said, "Well, yes, but only once."

"Once is all it takes," he replied.

Then the torso appeared and it was yellow. "Ma'am, have you ever slept with a Japanese?" the doctor asked.

"Well, yes," she said, "but only once."

"Once is all it takes," he said.

When the legs appeared they were red. The doctor asked her if she had ever slept with a Red Indian and she said, "Only once," and he replied that once was all it took.

Then the doctor held it upside down and slapped its bottom to make it cry.

"Oh, thank God," she exclaimed as the baby cried, "at least it doesn't bark!"

## Randy Dandy

At a big cocktail party, an obstetrician's wife noticed another guest – a big, oversexed Sardarni – was making overtures at her husband. But it was a large, informal gathering, so she tried to laugh it off, until she saw them disappear into a bedroom together.

At once she rushed into the room, pulled the two apart and screamed, "Look, lady! My husband just delivers babies, he doesn't INSTALL them!"

## Transferred Labour

A couple went to the hospital to have a baby. The doctor told them that he had invented a new machine that would automatically transfer a portion of the mother's labour pain to the father. He asked if the husband was willing to try it out.

Both the husband and wife were very much in favour of it. So the doctor set the knob at 10% for starters, explaining that even 10% was probably more pain than the father had ever experienced before. But, as labour progressed, the doctor adjusted the machine to 20% pain transfer.

The husband was still feeling fine. The doctor checked the husband's blood pressure and pulse and was amazed at how well he was doing. At this, they decided to try for 50%. The husband continued to feel quite well. Since it was obviously helping out his wife considerably, he encouraged the doctor to transfer ALL the pain to him.

The wife delivered a healthy baby with virtually no pain. She and her husband were ecstatic.

When they got home that afternoon, they found the milkman dead on the porch!

❏❏❏

# Sex Therapists' Tricks

## Little Games

"I'm worried," said the woman to her sex therapist. "I happened to find my daughter and the little boy next door both naked and examining each other's bodies."

"That's not unusual," smiled the therapist. "I wouldn't worry about it."

"But I am worried, doctor," insisted the woman, "and so is my daughter's husband!"

☺  ❖  ☺

## Hand Control

This guy goes into a doctor's clinic and says, "Doctor, doctor, you've got to help me. I just can't stop having sex!"

"Well, how often do you have it?" the doctor asks.

"Well, twice a day I have sex with my wife, TWICE a day," he answers.

"That's not so much," says the doctor.

"Yes, but that's not all. Twice a day I have sex with my secretary, TWICE a day," replies the man.

"Well, that is probably a bit excessive," says the doctor.

"Yes, but that's not all. Twice a day I have sex with a prostitute, TWICE a day," says the man.

"Well, that's definitely too much," says the doctor. "You've got to try and control yourself – take yourself in hand."

"I do," says the man. "Twice a day!"

## Come Again...

Dear doctor, both my wife and I are sterile. Is there any possibility that we will pass this on to our children?

Letter to a Sex Advisor in a cheesecake magazine's column:

Dear doctor, my husband and I have two children and would love to have another. But I read that every third child born is a Chinese. Considering we are Indians, do you think we should take the risk?

## Elderly Capers

An elderly couple visited a sex therapist and said: "We're having some trouble with our sex life. Could you watch and offer some suggestions?"

After watching them have sex, the doctor said, "You don't seem to be having any trouble. I wish my sex life was as good. I can't give you any suggestions."

This was repeated the next week and also the third week as the couple kept returning. After they had finished on the third week, the doctor said, "You aren't having any trouble. So why do you come to me. Is this your idea of kinky sex?"

The man replied, "No, actually the problem is that if we have sex at my house, my wife will catch us. If we have sex at her house, her husband will catch us. The guesthouse charges Rs 1,000 and we can't afford that. You only charge Rs 500 and Mediclaim reimburses half of that!"

## Beep Beep

An 83-year-old man married a vivacious 19-year-old college girl. He was quite content, but after a few weeks, she told him she was going to leave him if she didn't get some satisfying sex real soon. So the man went to a sex therapist, who then gave him a very high-priced shot of spermatozoa extracted from the rare Siberian roadrunner; the treatment cost Rs 60,000.

"Now look," said the doctor. "The only way you're going to get it hard is to say 'beep', and then to get it soft again, you say 'beep beep'."

"Excellent!" the old man said.

"Yes, but I must warn you," the doctor said, "it will only work three times in your life and then the spermatozoa tire out and die. And we don't have any more of this spermatozoa extract. The Siberian roadrunner has been extinct for over a decade now."

On his way home, the old man decided that he wasn't going to live through three bouts of sex anyway, so he decided to waste one of the beeps to try it out. "Beep!" he said. Immediately, his tool got hard and turned itself into a huge erection. Satisfied that it worked, he then said, "Beep! Beep!" and his organ got soft again. The old man chuckled with delight and anticipation.

Having lost his attention while driving momentarily and veering into another lane, a car next to him went "Beep!" and the car behind him also responded with "Beep! Beep!" Realising that these sounds had used up his second erection, the man raced home and ran into the house as fast as he could for his last great bang.

"Honey!" he shouted at his young wife. "Don't ask any questions. Just drop your clothes and hop into bed."

The old man nervously undressed and hollered "Beep!" which instantly gave him a large ten-inch erection. Caught up in his excitement, she stripped off all her clothes and jumped on the bed smiling with delight as she eyed his swollen member.

Then, just as he was about to get going, the young wife asked, "Alright! Now we're really smoking! But what's all this 'beep beep' shit?"

## Experimental Travails

A woman walks into her sex therapist's office and says that her husband is not a very good lover and they never have sex anymore and asks what can be done about it. The therapist tells her that he has an experimental drug that might do the trick. He tells the woman to give her husband one pill that night and come back in the morning and tell him what happened.

The next day, the woman comes in ecstatic telling the therapist that the pill worked and she and her husband had the best sex ever. She asks her therapist what would happen if she gave her husband two pills and the therapist says he doesn't know, but to go ahead and try it.

The next day, the same thing happens, the woman comes in telling the therapist that the sex was even better than the night before and what would happen if she gave him five pills. The therapist says he doesn't know, but to go ahead and try it.

The next day, the woman comes in limp but happy, and tells the therapist that the sex just keeps getting better and what would happen if she gave her husband the rest of the bottle. The therapist says he doesn't know, but it's worth a try.

So the woman leaves the therapist's office and puts the rest of the bottle of pills in the husband's morning coffee.

A week later, a boy walks into the therapist's office and says: "Are you the dumb jerk who gave my mother a bottle of experimental pills?"

"Why, yes, young man, I did. What's the matter?"

"Well, mom's dead, sister's pregnant, my butt hurts, and dad's sitting in the corner telling the cat, 'Here kitty, here kitty, here kitty…'."

## Nympho Blues

This guy took his nymphomaniac wife to the sex therapist for treatment. "This is one hot potato of a lady, doctor," he said. "Maybe you can do something for her. She goes for any man, any age, any time, any where… and it is just driving me crazy with jealousy."

"We'll see," the therapist said. He directed the wife into his examining room, closed the door behind her and told her to get undressed. Then he told her to get up onto the examining table on her stomach. The moment he touched her butt, she began to squirm and moan. It was too much for him to resist, so he climbed on top and began humping her.

The husband suddenly heard moans coming from the examination room. Very suspicious, he burst into the room and was confronted by the sight of the doctor astride his wife. "Doctor, what are you doing?" he yelled.

Flustered, the therapist replied, "Oh, it's you! I'm only taking your wife's temperature!"

The husband pulled out a large pocket-knife and began to hone it deliberately on his sleeve. "Well, doc," he said, "when you take that thing out, it better have numbers on it!"

## Dead Beat

A guy went to his doctor full of anger. "Doc," he said, "I feel like killing my wife. You've got to help me. Please tell me what I should do."

The doctor thought for a moment. "Look," he said, "here are some pills. Take these twice a day and they'll allow you to screw your wife six times a day. If you do this for 30 days, you'll finally screw her to death. And the autopsy will just show that she died of heart failure during sex."

"Wonderful, doc," said the grateful patient. "I'll start with this right away."

He left with the bottle of pills and a smile on his face. Nearly a month passed. One day, while on a medical convention, the doctor passed by the patient coming down the sidewalk in a wheelchair, just barely managing to move forward. "What happened?" asked the doctor. "What happened to your wife?"

"Don't worry, doc," the patient reassured him. "Two more days and she'll be dead."

## Pickle Slicer

Bholu worked in a pickle factory. He had been employed there for a number of years when he came home one day to confess to his wife that he had a terrible compulsion. He had an urge to stick his organ into the pickle slicer! His wife suggested he should see a sex therapist to talk about it, but Bholu said he'd be too embarrassed. He vowed to overcome the compulsion on his own.

One day a few weeks later, Bholu came home absolutely ashen. His wife could see at once that something was seriously wrong. "What's wrong, Bholu?" she asked.

"Do you remember I told you how I had this tremendous urge to put my dick into the pickle slicer?"

"Oh, Bholu, you didn't!"

"Yes, I did!"

"My God, Bholu! What happened?"

"I got fired."

"No, Bholu. I mean, what happened with the pickle slicer?"

"Oh... she got fired too!"

## Hot Shot

The couple visited a sex clinic to complain that their sex life had become a bore. Each night, the man would arrive home. His wife would prepare supper. After supper, they'd watch two hours of television. Immediately afterwards, they would go to bed. From that point on, every move was routine.

"No wonder," the sex therapist said. "You've made sex monotonous. Stop living on a schedule. Get into sex whenever you feel like it. Don't wait until bedtime each night to do it. Do it whenever you get into the mood."

The couple agreed to try the advice. They returned the following week. "How did things work out?" the therapist asked.

The man and his wife were beaming. "It worked great!"

"Tell me about it," said the therapist.

"Well, two nights after we saw you last, we were eating supper when I noticed that although it was only seven o'clock, I had this huge erection that was unstoppable. Sweetie pie here was staring at it with longing eyes. So I didn't wait for any shower or anything. Instead, I reached out, ripped off her blouse and bra. Then I tore off her panties. I flung her right onto the table, spilling all the wine and soup in the process. Then I unzipped my fly and pulled out my dick and we began. Man, we made love like we never had before!"

"That's wonderful!" said the sex therapist. "I told you it would work if you did it when the spirit moved you!"

"Only one thing," said the man a little sadly. "They're never ever going to let us go back to the restaurant at The Oberoi Hotel any longer."

## Gender Drill

This guy decides to get a sex change. So he goes to the doctor and has the thing done. A couple of weeks later he was talking to one of his old buddies about it. "Jeez, it must have really hurt when they shot all that silicon into your chest to make your breasts."

"Not really, I hardly felt it."

"Well, it must have really hurt when they chopped off your manhood!"

"Nope, I didn't really feel it either. The only thing that really hurt was when they drilled a hole in my skull and sucked out half my brain."

*A sperm donor's nightmare!*

## Vicarious Pleasure

There was a horrible mistake at the hospital. A man who was scheduled for a vasectomy was instead given a sex change operation. The doctors gathered at his bed afterwards to tell him the bad news. "Oh no!" the patient wailed. "I'll never be able to experience an erection again!"

"Of course, you'll still be able to experience erections," replied one surgeon, "only it will be someone else's!"

## Colour Counts

Ranchod went to the sex therapist one day and said, "Doc, I have a problem. My tool is red."

The doctor replied, "Drop your pants, let me take a look. Ummm... yes, no problem, we can have you fixed up in no time for 100 bucks."

The fellow was impressed. He told his friend of the experience and that he hadn't been to a doctor for only 100 bucks for quite a long time. His friend said, "Really? I have a similar problem."

So his friend went to the same doctor and told him, "Doc, Ranchod recommended you... you've got to help me. My organ is blue."

The doc says he'll take a look. "Ah yes... Ummm... Yes, we can take care of it, no problem, 1,000 bucks."

"One thousand rupees! Wait a MINUTE! You took care of Ranchod for only 100 bucks."

"Yes, I did. But Ranchod's organ had lipstick on it! Yours has gangrene."

## Condemned Colour

A sailor once ran into this sex therapist's office and begged for help. He pulled down his pants and showed the doctor his dick, which was sporting a ruby red ring around the tip. He asked the doctor if there was any cure for this strange VD. The doctor just smiled, soaked a cloth in alcohol and rubbed the end of his dick thrice. The sailor looked down and saw that the ring was gone. Ecstatic, he paid the doctor and ran off to catch his ship.

A few months later, another sailor came to the doctor and said: "A few months ago, my buddy came here with a ring around his dick and he said you just rubbed it thrice and he was cured. Well, I have a similar problem..."

The sailor pulled down his pants and showed his dick, which was sporting an emerald green ring around the tip.

Well, the doctor just reached into his pocket, took out a large knife and with one whack cut off the sailor's dick.

"What did you do that for?!" screamed the sailor in agony.

"Well, your buddy had lipstick around his dick," explained the doctor. "You had gangrene."

## Hair Splitting

A woman was going to marry one of those guys who want a virgin. Since she was not, she went to a doctor to reconstruct her hymen. The doctor told her that it would cost around Rs 5,000, but there was another way that would cost only Rs 500. The woman agreed to try the cheap way, paid the money and the doctor worked on her for several minutes.

After the "first night" of intimacy, the woman came back to the doctor and told him that it was perfect. The pain, the blood, everything was there. And she asked him how he did it.

"It was simple," he answered. "I just tied your pubic hair together."

## Hubby's List

A man is having problems with his dick, which certainly had seen better times... He consults a doctor who, after a couple of tests, says, "Sorry, but you've overdone it the past 30 years and your dick is burned out; you won't be able to make love more than 30 times!"

The man walks home deeply depressed. His wife is already expecting him at the front door and asks him what the doctor said concerning his problem. He tells her what the doc told him.

She says: "Oh my god – only 30 times! We should not waste that; we should make a list!"

He replies, "Yes, I already made a list on the way home; sorry my dear, your name is not on it!"

## Home-grown Trouble

A man returns to the doctor after having some tests and asks what the results were. The doctor explains that he has some bad news. In fact, the patient is HIV positive.

"Damn!" says the man. "You can't trust anybody nowadays, not even your own kids!"

## Taste-n-Tell

A Jewish boy was walking with his girlfriend on the grounds of his father's house. His father was a successful sex surgeon and was carrying out a circumcision at his on-site surgery. As they were walking, they heard a scream and a foreskin flew out of the window and landed at the girl's feet.

"What's this," she asked.

"Taste it," he replied. "If you like it, I'll give you a whole one!"

## Lady's Problem

A man walked into a therapist's office looking very depressed, "Doc, you've got to help me. I can't go on like this."

"What's the problem?" the doctor inquired.

"Well, I'm 35 years old and I still have no luck with the ladies. No matter how hard I try, I just seem to scare them away."

"My friend, this is not a serious problem. You just need to work on your self-esteem. Each morning, I want you to get up and run to the bathroom mirror. Tell yourself that you are a good person, a fun person and an attractive person. But say it with real conviction. Within a week you'll have women buzzing all around you."

The man seemed content with this advice and walked out of the office excited.

Three weeks later he returned with the same downtrodden expression on his face. "Did my advice not work?" asked the doctor.

"It worked alright. For the past several weeks I've enjoyed some of the best moments in my life with the most fabulous looking women."

"So, what's your problem?"

"I don't have a problem," the man replied. "My wife does!"

## Outsize

The young man went to the doctor, complaining of an awful lisp. Giving him a thorough examination, the doctor determined that his problem was the size of his 16-inch member; being so large, it was actually pulling his tongue off centre. Performing an emergency operation, the physician shortened the organ and sent the man on his way.

Several weeks later, the patient returned, complaining that while his lisp was gone, his sex life had also gone! "I'd like my organ back," he said mournfully.

At this, the doctor looked him straight in the eye and said, "Thcrew you. Not potthible!"

## D-Night

A sex therapist was delivering a lecture at the Gymkhana Club. "How many of you guys make love to your wives every night?" he asked.

A few men raised their hands.

"Twice a week?" he asked. A few more raised their hands.

"Once a month?" Still more hands.

"Only once a year?"

A man in the back row jumped up and eagerly shouted: "Me!"

"But why are you so cheerful about it?" inquired the therapist.

"Because tonight's the night!" gushed the man.

## Growing Organ

A man walks into a doctor's office and the doctor tells him, "I've got some good news and some bad news."

"Tell me the good news first," the patient says.

"The good news is that your tool is going to be two inches longer and an inch wider," the doctor replies.

"That's great!" says the patient. "What's the bad news?"

The doctor frowns, "It's malignant."

## Peeping Tom

A woman went to her sex therapist because she was having severe problems with her sex life. The therapist asked her many questions but did not seem to be getting a clear picture of her problems. Finally he asked, "Do you ever watch your husband's face while you are making love?"

"Well, yes, I did once."

"Well, how did he look?"

"Very angry."

At this point the therapist felt that he was really getting somewhere and said, "Well, that's very interesting; we must look into this, further. Now tell me, you say that you have only seen your husband's face once during sex; that seems somewhat unusual. Why was it that you saw his face at this time?"

"Because he was looking at us through the window!"

*Mr Solkar, the tests show you're not impotent. Your organ is just scared to death!*

## Startling Trouble

A man was having problems with premature ejaculation so he decided to go to the sex therapist. He asked the doctor what could be done to cure his problem.

In response, the doctor said, "When you feel like you are getting ready to ejaculate, try startling yourself."

That same day the man went to the store and bought himself a starter pistol. All excited to try this suggestion, he runs home to his wife. At home his wife is in bed, naked and waiting for him. As the two begin, they find themselves in the '69' position. Moments later, the man feels the sudden urge to come and fires the starter pistol.

The next day, the man went back to the doctor. The doctor asked, "How did it go?"

The man answered, "Not that well... when I fired the pistol, my wife crapped on my face, bit three inches off my tool and our neighbour came out of the almirah naked, with his hands in the air!"

# Viagra Tales

## Cool Use

A man goes to visit his 85-year-old grandpa in hospital. "How are you grandpa?" he asks.

"Feeling fine," says the old man.

"What's the food like?"

"Terrific, wonderful menus."

"And the nursing?"

"Just couldn't be better. These young nurses really take care of you."

"What about sleeping? Do you sleep OK?"

"No problem at all, nine hours' solid sleep every night. At 10 o'clock they bring me a cup of hot chocolate and a Viagra... and that's it. I go out like a light."

The grandson is puzzled and a little alarmed by this, so he rushes off to question the head nurse. "What are you people doing," he says. "I'm told you're giving an 85-year-old man Viagra on a daily basis. Surely that can't be true?"

"Oh, yes!" replies the nurse. "Every night at 10 o'clock we give him a cup of chocolate and a Viagra. It works wonderfully well. The chocolate makes him sleep, and the Viagra stops him from rolling out of bed!"

Did You Hear…

- Worldwide, men are being warned not to take Viagra with nitrates after five gentlemen in India did so and changed the balance of power in the region.
- Generic Viagra is sold under the name Fix-a-Flat.
- New Viagra eye drops make you look hard.
- Viagra has been a big boon to 'stand-up' comedians.
- One man spent too much money on Viagra. Now, he's hard up!
- Did you hear about the first death from an overdose of Viagra? A man took 12 pills and his wife died!
- A man at the chemist store for his Viagra prescription grumbles about the Rs 750-per-pill price. Standing next to him, his wife voices a different opinion: "Oh, Rs 3,000/- per year isn't too bad!"
- …Then there was the man who got his Viagra tablet stuck in his throat and suffered from a stiff neck.
- Have you tried the new hot beverage, Viagraccino? One cup and you're up all night.
- The Viagra computer virus turns your floppy disk into a hard drive. The Viagra super virus then sucks all your data off the hard drive.
- A guy left his Viagra tablet in the shirt pocket when he sent it to the laundry. Now, his shirt is too stiff to wear.
- News reports say it is no longer necessary for gardeners to stake tomatoes and other creepers. Just dissolve a Viagra tablet in the water and they stand up straight and tall.
- Viagra is now being compared to Disneyland — a one-hour wait for a 2-minute ride.

- Men taking iron supplements are warned that taking Viagra may cause them to spin around and point north!
- Rumour has it that when a truck carrying a load of Viagra slid off into the Ohio River, all the lift bridges suddenly went up.
- New plans are being made to raise the Titanic. Experts plan to pump it full of Viagra and expect it to rise right up.
- The difference between Niagara and Viagra? Niagara Falls!
- For years the medical profession has been looking after the ill, to make them better. Now, with Viagra, they're raising the dead!
- A Viagra delivery truck was hijacked: The police are looking for two 'hardened criminals'. They expect a stiff penalty under the penal code.
- Unconfirmed but frequent reports tell us that a man who overdosed on Viagra caused the funeral home problems — they couldn't close his coffin lid for three days.
- Even so, we're told that the funeral home industry is happy about Viagra overdoses: Lots of new stiffs mean an upswing in business.
- Newsweek's comment on the trade name Microsoft®: Let's see… "Micro" and "Soft". Needs Viagra!
- It has been revealed that criminals who steal Viagra will face stiff sentencing.
- What is the generic name for Viagra? Mycoxafillin….
- How can you tell if a man hasn't been taking his Viagra? It's not hard.
- What happens when you give Viagra to a lawyer? They get taller.
- How do you get Viagra from the Internet? All you need is a 3.5" floppy!

## Rising Tall

Two elderly men were talking about Viagra. One had never heard of it and asked the other what it was for. "It's the greatest invention ever," he said. "It makes you feel like a man of 30."

"Can you get it over the counter?"

"Probably — if you took two."

## Need-based Dose

A man was prescribed Viagra by his doctor who told him to take it one hour before sex. The man collected his prescription and went home to wait for his wife to get in from work. An hour before she was due home, he took the Viagra pill. But just as he was expecting her, she phoned to say that she wouldn't be in for another two and a half hours. In panic, he phoned the doctor. "What should I do?" he asked. "I've taken the pill but the effects will have worn off by the time my wife gets home."

"I see," said the doctor. "It is a pity to waste it. Do you have a maid?"

"Yes!"

"Well, could you not occupy yourself with her instead?"

"But I don't need Viagra with the maid!"

## Outdoors Fun

A man goes to a doctor and says, "Doctor, I have a sexual performance problem. Can you help me?"

"Oh, that's not a problem anymore!" announces the proud physician. "They just came out with this new wonder drug, Viagra, that does the trick! You take some pills and your problems are history." So the doctor gives the man a prescription and sends him on his merry way.

A couple of months later, the doctor runs into his patient on the street. "Doctor, doctor!" exclaims the man excitedly, "I've got to thank you! This drug is a miracle! It's wonderful!"

"Well, I'm glad to hear that," says the pleased physician. "And what does your wife think about it?"

"Wife?" says the man. "Hell! I don't know. I haven't gone home yet!"

# AIDS

## Chintu's Re-education

Chintu the homosexual goes into the doctor's office and has some tests done. The doctor comes back and says, "Chintu, I am not going to beat around the bush. You have AIDS."

Chintu is devastated. "Doc, what can I do?"

The doctor says, "I want you to go home and eat 5 pounds of spicy sausage, a head of cabbage, 20 unpeeled carrots drenched in hot sauce, 10 green chillies, 40 walnuts and 40 peanuts, ½ box of Kelloggs cereal and top it off with a litre of pineapple juice."

Chintu asks, "Will that cure me, doc?"

"No, but it should leave you with a better understanding of what your a***hole is meant for!"

## Sliding Solution

A man returns from a foreign holiday and is feeling very ill. He goes to see his doctor and is immediately rushed to the hospital to undergo tests.

The man wakes up after the tests in a private room at the hospital and the phone by his bed rings. "This is your doctor. We've had the results back from your tests and we've found you have an extremely nasty STD called G.A.S.H. It's a combination of Gonorrhoea, AIDS, Syphilis and Herpes!"

"Oh my gosh!" cries the man. "What are you going to do, doctor?"

"Well, we're going to put you on a diet of pizzas, pancakes and paranthas."

"Will that cure me?" asks the man.

The doctor replies, "Well no, but... it's the only food we can slide under the door."

## Pre-emptive Strike

A son takes his father to the doctor. The doctor gives them the bad news that the father is dying of cancer. The father tells the son that he has had a good long life and wants to stop at the bar on the way home to celebrate it.

While at the bar, the father sees several of his friends. He tells them that he is dying of AIDS.

When the friends leave, the son asks, "Dad, you are dying of cancer. Why did you tell them you are dying of AIDS?"

The father replies, "I don't want them screwing your mother after I'm gone!"

# Vet Antics

## The Best

Did you hear about the doctor who had his licence taken away because he was having affairs with his patients? It's a real shame because he was one of the top veterinarians in the country!

## Multi-city Business

Every Sunday, a little old lady placed Rs 10,000 in the collection plate during Mass. This went on for weeks until the priest, overcome with curiosity, approached her.

"Sister, I couldn't help but notice that you put Rs 10,000 a week in the collection plate," he stated.

"Why yes," she replied, "every week my son sends me money and what I don't need I give to the church."

"That's wonderful! How much does he send you?"

"Oh, Rs 20,000 a week."

"Your son seems very successful. What does he do for a living?"

"He is a veterinarian," she answered.

"That is a very honourable profession. Where does he practise?"

"Well, he has one cathouse in Falkland Road and branches at Foras Road (Mumbai), G.B. Road (Delhi) and Sonagachi (Kolkata)."

## Unwelcome Moves

Bunty took his Alsatian to the vet. "Doctor," he said, "I need you to cut off my dog's tail."

The vet was taken aback, "Bunty, why should I do such a terrible thing?"

"Because my mother-in-law's arriving tomorrow and I don't want anything to make her think she's welcome."

## The Dear Vet

A lady rushes into the veterinarian's clinic and screams, "I found my dog unconscious and I can't wake him – do something."

The vet puts the dog on the examination table and after a few simple tests he says, "I'm sorry, I don't feel a pulse, I'm afraid your dog is dead."

The lady can't accept this and says, "No, no, he can't be dead – do something else."

So the vet calls out, "Tommy!" A Labrador then comes bounding in. Going over to the table, the huge dog starts sniffing the dead dog all over. A minute later, he shakes his head and walks out.

"Well, that confirms it," the vet says. "Your dog is dead."

The lady is very upset and insists on a third opinion.

The vet goes into the other room and comes back with a little cat. The cat jumps up on the table and starts sniffing the dog from head to toe. It sniffs and sniffs up and down the dog, then all of a sudden just stops and jumps off the table and leaves.

"There," says the vet, "that reconfirms it."

The lady finally accepts the decision, although she's still upset. "Okay, I guess you're right. How much do I owe you?"

The vet says, "That will be Rs 3,500."

The lady has a fit and asks, "Why is it so much? After all you didn't do anything for the dog."

"Well," the vet replies, "it's Rs 500 for my consultation, Rs 1,000 for the Lab Test and Rs 2,000 for the Cat Scan!"

## Mercy Killing

A veterinarian was feeling ill and went to see her doctor. The doctor asked her all the usual questions, about symptoms, how long had they been occurring, etc, when she interrupted him: "Hey look, I'm a vet — I don't need to ask my patients these kind of questions. I can tell what's wrong just by looking. Why can't you?"

The doctor nodded, looked her up and down, wrote out a prescription, handed it to her and said, "There you are. Of course, if that doesn't work, we'll have no option but to have you put down."

# Optical Illusions

## Optometric Tricks

An optometrist was instructing a new employee on how to charge a customer: "As you are fitting his glasses, if he asks how much they cost, you say, '750 bucks.' If his eyes don't flutter, say... 'For the frames. The lenses will be 1,000 bucks.' If he still doesn't bat an eyelid, you add... 'Each.'"

## Spot Man

A man goes to the eye specialist. The receptionist asks him why he is there. The man complains, "I keep seeing spots in front of my eyes."

The receptionist asks, "Have you ever seen a doctor?"

The man replies: "No, no doctor, just spots!"

## Another Spot Man

Patient: "I always see spots before my eyes."

Doctor: "Didn't the new glasses help?"

Patient: "Sure, now I see the spots much clearer."

## Eye Sore

There was a world-famous painter who, in the prime of her career, began losing her eyesight. Fearful that she might lose her living as a painter, she went to see the best eye surgeon in the world.

After several weeks of delicate surgery and therapy, her eyesight was restored. The painter was so grateful that she decided to show her gratitude by repainting the doctor's office. Part of her work included painting a gigantic eye on one wall.

When she had finished her work, she held a press conference to unveil her latest work of art at the doctor's office. During the press conference, one reporter noticed the eye on the wall and asked the doctor, "What was your first reaction upon seeing your newly-decorated office, especially that one large eye on the wall?"

To this, the eye specialist responded, "I said to myself 'Thank the Lord, I'm not a gynaecologist!'"

# Doctors' Mixed Bag

## Coloured Pills

After the examination, a doctor explained his prescription: "Take the green pill with a glass of water after getting up. Take the blue pill with a glass of water after lunch. Just before bedtime, take the red pill with another glass of water."

Patient: "Doctor just what's wrong with me?"

Doctor: "You're not getting enough water!"

## Bang On

A young doctor had moved out to a small community to replace a doctor who was retiring. The older gent suggested the young one accompany him on his rounds so the community could become used to the new doctor. At the first house, a woman complained, "I've been a little sick in the stomach."

The older doctor said, "Well, you've probably been overdoing the fresh fruit. Why not cut back on the amount you've been eating and see if that does the trick?"

As they left the younger man said, "You didn't even examine that woman. How'd you come to your diagnosis so quickly?"

"I didn't have to. You noticed I dropped my stethoscope on the floor in there? When I bent over to pick it up, I noticed half-a-dozen banana peels in the trash. That was what was probably making her sick."

"Huh," the younger doctor said. "Pretty clever. I think I'll try that at the next house."

Arriving at the next house, they spent several minutes talking with an elderly woman. She complained that she just didn't have the energy she once did. "I'm feeling terribly run down lately."

"You've probably been doing too much work for the church," the younger doctor told her. "Perhaps you should cut back a bit and see if that helps."

As they left, the elder doctor said, "Your diagnosis is almost certainly correct, because she is heavily into church activities. But how did you arrive at it?"

"Well, just like you did at the last house, I dropped my stethoscope. When I bent down to retrieve it, I noticed the parish priest under the bed!"

## Spot Cure

A woman went to the doctor's office. She was seen by one of the new doctors, but after about four minutes in the examination room, she burst out screaming and ran down the hall. An older doctor stopped and asked her what the problem was and she explained. He then made her sit down and relax in another room.

The older doctor marched back to the new doctor and demanded, "What's the matter with you? Mrs Tambe is 63 years old, she has four grown children and seven grandchildren and you told her she was pregnant?"

The new doctor smiled smugly as he continued to write on his clipboard. "Cured her hiccups though, didn't it?"

## Dirty Mind

Dr Dharker, the biology instructor at a posh suburban girl's junior college, said during class, "Miss Sharma, would you please name the organ of the human body that, under the appropriate conditions, expands to six times its normal size, and define the conditions."

Miss Sharma gasped, blushed deeply, then said icily, "Dr Dharker, I do not think this is a proper question to ask me; you should be asking a boy. And I assure you my parents and the principal will hear of this." With that she sat down, very red-faced.

Unperturbed, Dr Dharker asked Miss Menon the same question. Calmly, Miss Menon replied, "The pupil of the eye, in dim light."

"Correct," said Dr Dharker. "And now, Miss Priya Sharma, I have three things to say to you. One, you have not studied your lesson. Two, you have a dirty mind. And three, you will some day – particularly on your wedding night – be faced with a dreadful disappointment!"

## Mum-cum-Dad

A woman starts dating a doctor. Before too long, she becomes pregnant and they don't know what to do.

About nine months later, just about the time she is going to give birth, a priest goes into the hospital for a prostate gland infection. The doctor says to the woman, "I know what we'll do. After I've operated on the priest, I'll give the baby to him and tell him it was a miracle."

"Do you think it will work?" she asks the doctor.

"It's worth a try," he says.

So, the doctor delivers the baby and then operates on the priest. After the operation he goes in to the priest and says, "Father, you're not going to believe this."

"What?" asks the priest. "What happened?"

"You gave birth to a child."

"But that's impossible!"

"I just did the operation," insists the doctor. "It's a miracle! Here's your baby."

About 15 years go by and the priest realises he must tell his son the truth some day or the other. One day he sits the boy down and says, "Son, I have something to tell you. I'm not your father."

The son says, "What do you mean, you're not my father?"

The priest replies, "I'm your mother! The archbishop is your father."

## Drug Speak

A man was just coming out of anaesthesia after a series of tests in the hospital and his wife was sitting at his bedside. His eyes fluttered open and he murmured, "You're beautiful."

Flattered, the wife continued her vigil while he drifted back to sleep. Later, her husband woke up and said, "You're cute."

Startled, she asked him, "What happened to 'beautiful'?"

"Oh!" he replied, "the drugs are wearing off."

## Poker Con

The doctor answered the phone and heard the familiar voice of a colleague on the other end of the line. "We need a fourth player for poker," said the friend.

"I'll be right over," whispered the doctor.

As he was putting on his coat, his wife asked, "Is it serious?"

"Oh yes, very serious," said the doctor gravely. "Why there are three doctors there already!"

## Left, Right & Centre

One day, in line at the company cafeteria, Ramit says to Mohit behind him, "My elbow hurts like hell. I guess I better see a doctor."

"Listen, you don't have to spend that kind of money," Mohit replies. "There's a diagnostic computer at the medical store on the corner. Just give it a urine sample and the computer will tell you what's wrong and what to do about it. It takes 10 seconds and costs 10 bucks only – a lot cheaper than a doctor."

So Ramit deposits a urine sample in a jar and takes it to the medical store's computer. He deposits ten bucks and the computer lights up and asks for the urine sample. He pours the sample into the slot and waits. Ten seconds later the computer ejects a printout: You have tennis elbow. Soak your arm in warm water and avoid heavy activity. It will improve in two weeks.

That evening, while thinking how amazing this new technology was, Ramit began wondering if the computer could be fooled. He mixed some tap water, a stool sample from his dog, urine samples from his wife and daughter and jacked off into the mixture for good measure.

Then Ramit hurried back to the medical store, eager to check the results. He deposited ten bucks, poured in his concoction, and awaited the results.

The computer printed the following:

1. Your tap water is too hard. Get a water softener.
2. Your dog has ringworm. Get an anti-fungal shampoo and bathe him with it.
3. Your daughter is addicted to opium. Get her into a rehabilitation centre.
4. Your wife is pregnant... twin girls. They aren't yours. Get a lawyer.
5. If you don't stop your hand practice and continue jacking off, your tennis elbow will never get better.

## Earful of Trouble

A man with two badly burned ears went to the emergency room for medical treatment. "What happened?" asked the doctor.

"Well, my wife was ironing while I was watching the one-day match on TV," began the man. "She put the hot iron near the telephone and when the phone rang, I answered the iron!"

The doctor nodded, "But what happened to the other ear?"

"Well, it was a wrong number. No sooner had I hung up on the previous call," said the man, "when the same guy called again."

## Memory Quirks

Two elderly couples were enjoying a friendly conversation when one of the men asked the other, "Rustam, how was the memory clinic you went to last month?"

"Outstanding," Rustam replied. "They taught us all the latest psychological techniques: visualisation, association, etc. It was great."

"That's great! And what was the name of the clinic?"

Rustam went blank. He thought and thought, but couldn't remember. Then a smile broke across his face and he asked, "What do you call that flower with a long stem and thorns?"

"You mean a rose?"

"Yes, that's it!"

Calling out to his wife, Rustam asked: "Rose, what was the name of that memory clinic?"

## Final Count

Mukri goes to the doctor's office complaining of not feeling well. The doctor runs some tests on him and returns in a few minutes. "Mukri, sit down. I've some bad news. You don't have much time to live."

Mukri is obviously upset about this, but asks, "How much longer do I have?"

The doctor says, "10."

Mukri says, "10 what? 10 weeks... 10 months... 10 years?"

The doctor replies, "10... 9... 8... 7..."

## Shoe Bites

A guy stops by to visit his friend who is paralysed from the waist down. They talk for a while and then the friend asks, "My feet are cold. Would you be so kind as to go get me my shoes please?"

The guest obliges and goes upstairs. There he sees his friend's two daughters, both very good-looking. Being the adventurous and quick-thinking kind, he says: "Hi, girls! Your daddy sent me here to have sex with you!"

They stare at him and say, "That can't be true!"

He replies, "OK, let's check!"

He shouts at his friend down the stairs, "Both of them?"

"Yes, both of them!"

## Better Planning

The Queen of England was visiting one of Canada's top hospitals and during her tour of the floors she passed a room where a male patient was wanking off. "Oh my God!" exclaimed the Queen. "That's disgraceful! What is the meaning of this?"

The doctor replied, "That man has a very serious condition where the testicles rapidly fill with semen. If he doesn't do that thrice a day, they'll explode, and he would die instantly."

"Oh, I am sorry," said the Queen.

On the next floor they passed a room where a young nurse was giving a patient oral sex. "Oh my God!" said the Queen. "What's happening in there?"

The doctor replied, "Same problem, better health plan."

## Iron Shots

A village woman takes her three sons to the doctor for physicals for the first time in their lives. The doctor examines the boys and tells the woman that they are healthy but she needs to give them iron supplements. She goes home and wonders exactly what iron supplements are. Finally, she goes to the hardware store and buys iron ball bearings (BBs) and mixes them into their food.

Several days later the youngest son comes to her and tells her that he is pissing BBs. She tells him that it is normal because she had put them in his food. Later, the middle son comes to her and says that he is crapping BBs. Again, she says that it is okay.

That evening the eldest son comes in very upset. He says, "Mom, you won't believe what happened."

She says, "I know – you're passing BBs!"

"No," he says. "I was out behind the barn jacking off and I shot the dog."

## Bearer's Stone

Early one morning, Paul Bearer, who worked at the local funeral parlour, woke his wife, complaining of severe abdominal pains. They rushed to the emergency room at the local hospital, where they gave him a series of tests to determine the source of the pain.

Paul told his wife not to call in sick for him at his office, until they knew what was wrong. When the results came back, the nurse informed them that, true to their suspicions, he was suffering from a kidney stone.

Paul's wife turned to him and asked, "Would you like me to call the funeral parlour now?"

With an alarmed look, the nurse quickly said, "Ma'am, he's not THAT sick!"

## Taste-less

A man is urinating one day when the end of his organ drops off. He thinks: 'This is probably not a good thing,' so he picks up the knobby end and sticks it in his pocket, then races off to the doctor. He waits in the surgery for a while, then he's called in.

The doctor greets him and asks, "What's the problem?"

"Well, doctor, I was urinating and my knob fell off. Here it is." And he reaches into his pocket and hands the piece to the doctor.

The doctor looks, frowns, then replies, "What rubbish! This is a jamun!"

"That's not possible! I ate my last jamun on the way in here!"

☺ ❖ ☺

## Framed Show

A man decides to take the opportunity while his wife is away to paint the toilet seat. The wife comes home sooner than expected, sits, and gets the seat stuck to her rear. She is understandably distraught about this and asks her husband to drive her to the doctor. She puts on a large overcoat to cover the stuck seat, and they go.

At the doctor's clinic, the man lifts his wife's coat. "Doctor, have you ever seen anything like this before?"

"Well, yes," the doctor replies, "but not framed like that."

## Misleading Decor

A new office opened on Colaba Causeway. It had no sign on either the door or window. About the closest thing to any identification was a large clock in the window. This yuppie shopper stopped by and inquired about a new battery for his watch and the clerk said that he was sorry, but they didn't perform any watch repairs at all.

The yuppie said, "Well, what's the significance of that clock you have in your window?"

The clerk smiled and said, "This is a clinic for the Atmaram Trust Hospital. All we do here is prostate and haemorrhoid examinations. What would you have us put in the window?"

## Monty's Monotony

Monty complained to his friend Jonty that love-making with his wife was becoming routine and boring.

"Get creative Monty. Break the monotony. Why don't you try playing doctor for an hour? That's what I do," said Jonty.

"Sounds great," Monty replied. "But how do you make it last for an hour?"

"Hell, just keep her in the waiting room for 55 minutes!"

## Plain Speak

The man told his doctor he wasn't able to do all the things around the house that he used to do. When the examination was complete, he said, "Now, doc, I can take it. Tell me in plain English what is wrong with me."

"Well, in plain English," the doctor replied, "you're just plain lazy."

"Okay," said the man. "Now give me the medical term so I can tell my wife!"

## The Boss

When the Lord made man, all the parts of the body argued over who would be boss. The brain explained that since he controlled all the parts of the body, he should be boss. The legs argued that since they took man wherever he wanted to go, they should be boss. The stomach countered with the explanation that since he digested all the food, he should be boss. The eyes said that without them man would be helpless, so they should be boss.

Finally, it was the a***hole's turn. So the a***hole also applied for the job. The other parts of the body laughed so hard at this that the a***hole became mad and closed up.

After a few days…

The brain went foggy, the legs got wobbly, the stomach got ill, and the eyes got crossed and unable to see. They all conceded and made the a***hole boss.

This proves that you don't have to be a brain to be the boss… Just an a***hole!

## Beating Crap

A modest man was in the hospital for a series of test. One of the last tests had left his system upset. After making several trips to the bathroom on false alarms, he decided the latest was another. But he completely filled his bed up with human waste and was embarrassed like hell. Losing his presence of mind, he jumped up, gathered the bed sheets and threw them out of the hospital window.

Just then, a drunkard was walking by the hospital when the sheets landed on him. He started yelling, cursing and swinging his arms, which drew the attention of the security guard.

The security guard asked, "What's going on here?"

Replied the proud drunk, thumping his chest, "I just beat the shit out of a ghost!"

☺ ❖ ☺

## Coronary Rebound

A coroner was working late one night. It was his job to examine the dead bodies before they were sent off for burial or cremation. As he examined the body of Mr Lamba, who was about to be cremated, he made an amazing discovery: Lamba had the longest private part he had ever seen!

"I'm sorry, Mr Lamba," said the mortician, "but I can't send you off to be cremated with a tremendously huge private part like this. It has to be saved for posterity."

And with that the coroner used his tools to remove the dead man's organ. He then stuffed his prize into a briefcase and took it home.

The first person he showed it to was his wife. "I have something to show you that you won't believe," he said and opened his briefcase.

"Oh my!" she screamed. "Lamba is dead!"

☺ ❖ ☺

## Winning Hand

The patient went to his doctor for a check-up, and the doctor wrote out a prescription for him in his usual illegible writing. The patient put it in his pocket, but he forgot to take it to the chemist.

Every morning for the next two years, he showed it to the ticket checker as a railway pass. Twice, it got him into movie theatres, once into the cricket match, and once into the stage play. He got a raise at work by showing it to the Accounts Department as a note from the boss.

One day, he mislaid it. His daughter picked it up, played it on the piano, and won a scholarship to a conservatory of music.

## Oral Satiation

One night, as a couple are going to bed, the husband gently taps his wife on the shoulder and starts rubbing her arm. The wife turns over and says, "I'm sorry dear, I've got a gynaecologist appointment tomorrow and I want to stay fresh."

The rejected husband is still quite horny, but turns over and tries to sleep. A few minutes later, he rolls back over and taps his wife again. This time he whispers in her ear, "Do you have a dentist appointment tomorrow too?"

## Straight Talk

Doctor Pandey and his wife are having dinner at an upscale restaurant when an attractive young girl walks by, smiles at the doctor and says, "Hi Sharad!"

The wife, somewhat irritated, asks, "And who is that?"

The doctor says, "That's my mistress."

The wife asks, "You have a mistress? How long has this been going on?"

Dr Pandey: "About five years."

Wife: "Five years? I'll see a lawyer tomorrow and sue for divorce. You'll be ruined."

Dr Pandey: "Now think about it. If we divorce, we each get half of what we have. You won't have that big house, won't get a new car every year and won't be shopping and playing rummy all day long with your so-called friends."

Just then a cute lady walks by and says, "Hi Sharad!"

Wife: "And who is that one?"

Dr Pandey: "That's Dr Mehta's mistress."

Wife: "Doctor Mehta has a mistress too?"

Dr Pandey: "Since the past 12 years."

Wife: "Ours is a lot prettier."

# Merry Old Men

## Tool Threat

This old man in his eighties got up and was putting on his coat. His wife asks, "Where are you going?"

He says, "I'm going to the doctor."

And she says, "Why? Are you sick?"

"No," he replies, "I'm going to get some of those new Viagra pills."

So his wife gets off her butt, starts putting on her sweater and he asks, "Where are you going?"

She replies, "I'm going to the doctor, too."

He asks, "Why?"

She says, "If you're going to start using that rusty old thing again, I'm going to need a tetanus shot!"

## Sowing His Oats

An 80-year-old woman married an 85-year-old man. After about six months together, the woman wasn't feeling well and she went to her doctor.

The doctor examined her and said, "Congratulations Mrs Bandukwala! You're going to be a mother."

"Get serious doctor, I'm 80."

"I know," said the doctor. "This morning, I would have said it was impossible, but this afternoon you are a medical miracle."

"I'll be damned," she replied and stormed out of the office. She walked down the hall and around the corner to where the telephones were. In a rage, she dialled her husband, Mr Bandukwala.

"Hello!" she heard him say in his familiar halting voice on the other end. She screamed, "You rotten son of a gun, Bandukwala! You got me pregnant!"

There was a long pause on the line. Finally, her husband answered, "Who's calling please?"

## Boarding Fun

There was this 80-year-old man who was seeing the doctor for a check-up. The doctor asked why he needed the check-up. The man was getting married next month to a girl 60 years his junior. The doctor tried to talk him out of the marriage, but it didn't work. Finally, the doctor suggested, "If you want your marriage to last, I suggest you take in a boarder."

The old man agreed. He then didn't see the doctor for a year, until one day they met in the market. The old man said, "Doctor, congratulate me, my wife is pregnant!"

"That's good news," said the doctor. "I knew the boarder would help."

"Oh," said the old man with a wicked grin, "thanks for the tip about keeping a boarder. The boarder is pregnant too."

## Wrong Timings

Three old men are sitting on the porch of a retirement home. The first says, "Hey fellows! I got real problems. I'm 70 years old. Every morning at seven o'clock I get up and I try to urinate. All day long I try to urinate. They give me all kinds of medicine but nothing helps."

The second old man says, "You think you have problems. I'm 80 years old. Every morning at 8:00 I get up and try to move my bowels. I try all day long. They give me all kinds of stuff but nothing helps."

Finally, the third old man speaks up, "Fellows, that's nothing. I'm 90. Every morning at 7:00 sharp I urinate. Every morning at 8:00 sharp I move my bowels. Every morning at 9:00 sharp I wake up!"

## No-hoper

This 82-year-old man married a 22-year-old woman and they decided that they wanted to have kids. So after trying for a while with no success, he went to see the urologist, pretty discouraged. The urologist told him not to get discouraged and that they could conduct some tests.

"Take this specimen jar into the bathroom and leave me a specimen to test," the doctor said.

The old man closed the door and about an hour later, he had still not come out. The doctor came by and asked, "Are you alright?"

"No! This just isn't going to work," the old man dejectedly explained. "There's no hope for me. I've worn out my left hand, I've worn out my right hand, I've run cold water over it, and I've run hot water over it. I've even thumped it on the edge of the sink. But no way can I get the top off this specimen jar!"

## Lowered Sex Drive

An extremely old man visits his doctor. "Doctor, you must help me. I need my sex drive lowered."

The incredulous doctor says, "What? You want your sex drive lowered? But Mr Das, you have no sex drive! It's all in your mind."

To which the old man replies, "Exactly! It's all in my head! And I want it LOWERED!"

## Sex Organs, Please

A 90-year-old man announces his intention to marry a woman of 30. He is persuaded to have a medical exam first. "Everyone tells me I need a check-up to see if I'm sexually fit," he tells the doctor.

"Okay," says the medic, "let me see your sex organs."

So the old man sticks out his tongue and middle finger!

☺  ❖  ☺

## Lights On!

A doctor is making a routine call to one of his elderly patients. He asks, "And how are you doing today, Mr Ahmed?"

Ahmed replies, "I feel just fine, doc. But you know, it's the strangest thing. Every night when I get up to pee, the bathroom light comes on for me automatically when I open the door."

The doctor is worried that the old guy is getting senile, so he phones the man's son, and the son's wife answers. The doctor tells her, "Mrs Ahmed, I'm a little concerned about your father-in-law. It seems that when he gets up to urinate at night and opens the bathroom door, the light somehow comes on..."

Mrs Ahmed yells out to her husband, "Akram! Daddy's pissing in the refrigerator again!"

☺ ❖ ☺

## Special Check-up

An old man and his wife go to the doctor's clinic. The man who has a hearing problem is there for a physical, so the doctor tells the man he will need a urine and stool sample.

The man says, "Uuhh?"

The doctor repeats, "I will need a urine and stool sample."

"Uuhh?" This time the man looks at his wife and asks, "What did the doctor say?"

The wife answers in a loud voice, "He needs to check your underwear dear!"

☺ ❖ ☺

## Prescriptive Sex

The old man takes the old lady to the doctor for a check-up. The doctor wants to have some fun with the old man, so after the check-up he tells the old man that the problem is serious – the old lady's health is deteriorating and the only cure is sex.

The old man says, "Sex?"

"Yes," the doctor says, "sex you know!"

"How many times must she have sex?" the old man inquires.

The doctor says thrice a week.

"What days?" the old man asks.

"Well, let's say Tuesday, Thursday and Saturday," the doctor plays on.

"Well, doctor, Tuesday and Thursday are fine, but on Saturdays I have something to do and can't bring her to you on Saturdays!" the old man says.

☺ ❖ ☺

## Multiple Failure

There is this really old guy, around 80 years old. He comes into a hospital and says: "I want to donate some sperm."

So the nurse gives him a jar and tells him to come back tomorrow with the sperm.

The next day, he went back but the jar was empty. So, the nurse asks, "What happened? Where's the sperm?"

"Well," he replies, "I went home and tried so hard! I used my right hand and then my left hand. Then my wife tried! She used her right hand and then she tried her left hand! Then she used her mouth, once using her teeth and once without. Then we asked our neighbour to come over and she tried with her left hand and then her right hand! Then she tried with her mouth, once with her teeth and once without."

The nurse gasps. "Oh dear! You even asked your neighbour!"

The man says, "Yeah! And we still couldn't get the damn jar open!"

## Foreign Fire

An 80-year-old man is having his annual check-up. The doctor asks him how he's feeling. "I've never been better!" he replies. "I've got an 18-year-old bride who's pregnant and having my child! What do you think about that?"

The doctor considers this for a moment and says, "Well, let me tell you a story. I know a guy who's an avid hunter. He never misses a season. But one day he's in a hurry and he accidentally grabs his umbrella instead of his gun. So, he's in the jungle and suddenly a Himalayan bear appears in front of him! He raises his umbrella, points it at the bear and squeezes the handle. The bear drops dead in front of him."

"But that's impossible! Someone else must have shot that bear."

"Exactly!" smiles the doctor.

## Reverse Strength

An old man goes to the doctor to ask him an important question. "Doctor, when I was in my 20s, it took both of my hands to push down my hard-on. When I was in my 30s, it took one hand to push down my hard-on. When I was in my 50s, it took three fingers to push down my hard-on. Now that I'm in my 60s, it only takes one finger to push down on my hard-on!

"So what I'm basically trying to ask you is – how strong am I going to get?"

## Dress Rehearsal

An old woman went to visit her daughter and found her naked, waiting for her husband. The mother asks the daughter: "What are you doing naked?"

The daughter responds: "This is the dress of love."

When the mother returns home, she strips naked and waits for her husband. When her husband arrives, he asks her: "What are you doing naked, woman?"

She responds: "This is the dress of love."

So he retorts, "Well, then go iron it first!"

# Medical Limericks

## Spot Check
Before giving meds or IVs,
Be sure to check patient IDs.
    For the patient ahead
    May be in the wrong bed
While the right one is an absentee.

## Avoid the List
When giving your patients an assist,
Save your back. Avoid doing the twist.
    Beg, plead or yelp
    But round up some help.
Keep your name off the casualty list.

## Double Check
Give unusual orders a check.
Confirm them; make sure they're correct.
    It's O.K. to give rein
    And make use of your brain.
Remember, it's YOUR licence and neck.

## Tucked Right

When a "sundowner's" tucked in for the night
Be sure that his posey's tied tight.
    Or he'll wander around
    Till he finally falls down
And an incident report you must write.

## Preventive Belt

A booze-impaired patient named Ted
Refused to be posey'd in bed.
    The nurse said, in part,
    "The belt, you old fart,
Prevents falling and hitting your head!"

## Fighting Patient

If you waken a patient at night,
Please be gentle, don't give him a fright.
    And stand back from the bed.
    If he's out of his head,
He might try to punch out both your lights.

## Don't Ignore

Water or ice on the floor
Are things you should never ignore.
    The words you recite
    May not be polite
When you land on your posterior.

## Illegible Scrawl

Writing orders, a doctor from Flaster
Made his pen scribble faster and faster.
    He developed a scrawl
    That was unreadable.
And left his patients at risk for disaster!

## Eyestrain

Reviewing the charts is a pain.
Poor handwriting gives me eyestrain.
    By the end of the shift
    What I need is a lift,
Not further assault on my brain.

## Whack's Back!

When the monitor showed runs of V-tach,
The nurse gave Joe's sternum a whack.
    With a look of surprise,
    Old Joe opened his eyes.
Then he said, "My, it's good to be back!"

## Town Yell

Fred's catheter tubing hung down,
Off the bed, barely clearing the ground.
    Then his nurse, Cindy-Lou,
    Hooked the tube with her shoe.
Fred's yell was heard all over town!

## Randy Andy

Down with heart sickness
The nurse was his weakness.
    Since old man Andy
    Was horny and dandy
"Your tonic," the doc said, "is heady Ms Agnes."

## Sloan's Grown

There was a young dentist named Sloan,
Who catered to women alone.
    In an act of depravity,
    He filled the wrong cavity,
And said, "My, how my business has grown!"

## Muldoon at Noon

On Viagra was old man Muldoon,
When he went on his third honeymoon.
    Morning coffee was brewin',
    When he started screwin',
And he finished at twelve o'clock noon.

# The World of Assorted Medical Cracks

Four signs you may need a new doctor:
- ✦ You can read his handwriting.
- ✦ His malpractice lawyer names him "Client of the Year"!
- ✦ He asks you to turn your head and cough during an eye exam.
- ✦ During surgery he keeps repeating, "The thigh bone is connected to the knee bone"!

Figure This...
- ✦ Today 4 out of 5 doctors recommend another doctor.
- ✦ I stopped taking tranquillisers. I was starting to be nice to people I didn't even want to talk to.
- ✦ I stopped taking this new pill to increase virility. It backfired and I got piles!
- ✦ It always amazes me the progress scientists are making in cancer research. Every day they discover something else that causes it!

## What Do...

If tennis players get tennis elbow, and squash players get squash knees, what do gynaecologists get?

Tunnel vision!

What do puppies and near-sighted gynaecologists have in common?

They both have wet noses!

## Last Words

A South African doctor wrote about an epitaph he had seen in a local cemetery:

In memory of my father: gone to join his appendix, his tonsils, his olfactory nerve, a kidney, a eardrum, and a leg, prematurely removed by an intern who needed the experience.

## Double Quotes

James Bryce: "Medicine is the only profession that labours incessantly to destroy the reason for it's own existence."

Voltaire (1694-1778): "Doctors pour drugs of which they know little, to cure diseases of which they know less, into human beings of whom they know nothing."

Voltaire: "The art of medicine consists of amusing the patient while nature cures the disease."

Benjamin Franklin (1706-1790): "He's the best physician that knows the worthlessness of most medicines."

## Kinky Pregnancy Q&As

Should I have a baby after 35?
No, 35 children are enough!

I'm two months pregnant now. When will my baby move?
With any luck, right after s/he finishes college.

What is the most common pregnancy craving?
For men to be the ones who get pregnant!

What is the most reliable method to determine a baby's sex?
Childbirth.

The more pregnant I get, the more often strangers smile at me. Why?
Because you're fatter than they are!

My wife is five months pregnant and so moody that sometimes she's borderline irrational.
So what's your question?

My childbirth instructor says it's not pain I'll feel during labour, but pressure. Is she right?
Yes, in the same way that a cyclone might be called an air current.

Is there any reason I have to be in the delivery room while my wife is in labour?
Not unless the word "alimony" or "maintenance" means anything to you.

Is there anything I should avoid while recovering from childbirth?
Yes, pregnancy.

Our baby was born last week. When will my wife begin to feel and act normal again?

When the kid is in college.

## Doctor-speak

When the doctor says: "One of several things could cause your symptoms."

What the doctor means: "I haven't the foggiest idea what's wrong with you."

When the doctor says: "Are you certain you haven't had this before?"

What the doctor means: "Because now you've got it again."

When the doctor says: "I'd like to run that last test again."

What the doctor means: "The lab lost your sample."

When the doctor says: "This prescription has a few side effects."

What the doctor means: "You may experience sudden hair growth on your palms."

When the doctor says: "Your insurance should cover most of this."

What the doctor means: "You'll have to sell your house to cover the rest."

When the doctor says: "Let's go over your symptoms once more."

What the doctor means: "I can't remember who you are."

When the doctor says: "How long have you had these symptoms?"

What the doctor means: "How do you feel about living with them the rest of your life?"

When the doctor says: "This won't hurt much."

What the doctor means: "Did you bring a bullet to bite?"

When the doctor says: "There's a lot of this going around."

What the doctor means: "We'll give it a name as soon as we figure out what it is."

When the doctor says: "We'll just remove this ingrown toenail."

What the doctor means: "A cane and orthopaedic shoes should help."

## Hear This…

The difference between a neurotic and a psychotic is that, while a psychotic thinks that 2 + 2 = 5, a neurotic knows the answer is 4, but it worries him.

One mouse to another: "I've got three brothers in psychological testing and a sister in heart research."

Intern to patient: "Did you know that diarrhoea is hereditary?"

Patient: "Why, no."

Intern: "Yes, it runs in your genes."

My wife came home from the doctor's the other day and said that he told her she couldn't make love. Now I'm wondering how he found out!

My mom takes so many Iron tablets, the only time she feels good is when she's facing the magnetic north. My brothers are now fighting over her mineral rights!

Miracle drug: Anything that will do 25% as much as the label says.

Miracle drug: Anything the kids will take without screaming.

The doctor used so many medicines he didn't know which one worked!

An apple a day won't do it nowadays!

## Guess What…

- ✦ Hospital bills are now divided into parts and labour.
- ✦ If laughter were the best medicine doctors would find a way to charge for it.
- ✦ Virus is a Latin word for your guess is as good as mine.

- At today's prices, we need a good affordable disease.
- My artificial kidney got kidney stones.
- Germs attack the weakest part of your body – the head.
- Get-well cards are such fun people are trying to get sick more often.
- Modern-day prescription – take one pill as often as you can afford it.
- Side effect of new wonder drugs – Bankruptcy.
- Say what you want about managed health-care. It's given us more ulcers.
- We drink toasts to everyone else's health and ruin our own.
- If you can't cure it, insure it.
- A man's lament: My health insurance policy only pays if I get pregnant.
- This managed care movement is picking up steam. That's what happens when you're going downhill.
- Car dealers are your friends. Now have a new car-sickness pill. Take one before each payment.
- If you don't take some kind of pill your colleagues will think you're overconfident.
- What's the death rate? One to a person.
- My inner child was adopted.
- The new drugs are so exciting I feel like I'm missing something by being in good health.
- Drug abuse used to be two doses of castor oil.

## Double Takes

Thanks to the tremendous strides in medicine people are living longer. This gives them the extra time needed to pay their medical bills.

Nurse to patient: "Don't worry, the doctor has seen an operation exactly like yours on TV."

Doctor to patient: "It's not habit forming. I should know. I've been taking it for 12 years now!"

The doctor said to let him know how the prescription works because he's having the same problem himself.

Researchers have developed a medication that, when taken under doctor's orders, is guaranteed not to make your cold any worse.

Penicillin has been called the "wonder drug" because any time the doctor wonders what you have, that's what you get.

A lot of people who switched from cyclamates to saccharin got artificial diabetes.

To find out what your doctor recommends just watch TV. It's a lot cheaper.

A few weeks ago I was so run down I could barely spank the baby. After taking four bottles of your wonderful medicine, I can now thrash my husband in addition to my regular housework.

Sign seen on the door of a medical school building: Staph Only.

Did you hear about the two blood corpuscles named Romeo and Juliet? They loved in vein!

Then there is the joke about the homeopath who forgot to take his medicine and died of an overdose!

Have you heard about the new medication that's both an aphrodisiac and laxative? It's called: "Easy Come, Easy Go"!

## Medical bloopers reported from America:

- Many young girls enter the office complaining of "ministerial" trouble.
- Pain in the lower quadrants may be described as, "I think I'm having overly trouble."
- A woman told the doctor that she once had an abdominal operation, "They took out all my female organdies."

## Wisecracks

Scientists say that 90% of all one-rupee notes carry germs. Not true! Even a germ can't live on one buck these days.

Bombeck's Rule of Medicine: Never go to a doctor whose office plants have died.

Hospital Telephone Hotline: Rrrring, rrrring. "Hello, Breast Self-Exam Hotline! For assistance, please press one now. Now press the other one!"

The New England Journal of Medicine reports that 9 out of 10 doctors agree that 1 out of 10 doctors is an idiot.

It is said that the limbic system of the brain controls the four Fs: Feeding, Fighting, Fleeing, and Reproduction.

Signboard in the office of a Chinese doctor: Specialist in women and other diseases.

What is the difference between an oral and a rectal thermometer? The taste.

## Polish Delights

What does the M.D. after the name of a Polish physician stand for? Mentally deficient!

How can you determine that a death certificate was filled by a Polish doctor?

He signs his name under "cause of death".

What happened to the Russian call-girl who had an appendectomy performed by a Polish surgeon?

He sewed up the wrong hole, so now she's making money from the other side!

A Polish doctor gets a call from the Medicare office. "You've been billing us for weekly house calls to Mr Ivanov for the last six months. Haven't you noticed that Mr Ivanov has passed away?"

"Sure I noticed! He was my favourite patient. So I visit him at the cemetery."

A Polish man goes to a doctor. "What's bothering you?" the doctor asks.

"You charge a hundred dollars just for consultation and ask me what's bothering me? Figure out yourself!"

"You should have gone to a veterinarian. They figure out what's bothering patients who can't tell them."

A Polish man is forced to seek the doctor's advice because his breath smells terrible.

The doctor examines him and says: "Either stop biting your nails or stop scratching your piles."

Did you hear about the Polish man who told his doctor he contracted a venereal disease from a wet dream?

## More Wisecracks

How do you tell the difference between male chromosomes and female chromosomes? Pull down their genes!

"The doctor said he would have me on my feet in two weeks."

"And did he?"

"Yes, I had to sell the car to pay the bill."

A Mumbai physician has discovered a sure cure for nervousness in women. He tells them it's a sign of old age.

There's this doctor who is so conceited about his looks and charm that whenever he takes a woman's pulse, he subtracts 10 beats to account for her being excited near him!

From Harper's Index: Number of people who aren't doctors, but play them on TV: 57.

Number of people who aren't doctors, but play them in hospitals: 5,840.

## Record Blunders

- ✦ The skin was moist and dry.
- ✦ Rectal examination revealed a normal size thyroid.
- ✦ The patient had cornflakes for breakfast and anorexia for lunch.
- ✦ She stated that she had been constipated for most of her life until 1999, when she got a divorce.

- Between you and me, we ought to be able to get this lady pregnant.
- The patient was in his usual state of good health until his airplane ran out of gas and crashed.
- The lab test indicated abnormal lover function.
- The baby was delivered, the cord clamped and cut, and handed to the paediatrician, who breathed and cried immediately.
- Exam of genitalia reveals that he is circus sized.
- I saw your patient today, who is still under our car for physical therapy.
- Bleeding started in the rectal area and continued all the way to Apollo Hospital.
- She is numb from her toes down.
- Exam of genitalia was completely negative except for the right foot.
- While in the emergency room, she was examined, X-rated and sent home.
- The patient suffers from occasional, constant, infrequent headaches.
- Coming from Jabalpur, this man has no children.
- Examination reveals a well-developed male lying in bed with his family in no distress.
- Patient was alert and unresponsive.
- When she fainted, her eyes rolled around the room.
- By the time he was admitted, his rapid heart had stopped, and he was feeling better.
- Patient has chest pain if she lies on her left side for over a year.
- On the second day the knee was better and on the third day it had completely disappeared.
- The patient has been depressed ever since she began seeing me in 1993.

- ✦ Discharge status: Alive but without permission.
- ✦ The patient is tearful and crying constantly. She also appears to be depressed.
- ✦ Healthy-appearing decrepit 69-year-old male, mentally alert but forgetful.
- ✦ The patient refused an autopsy.
- ✦ The patient expired on the floor uneventfully.
- ✦ Patient has left his white blood cells at another hospital.
- ✦ The patient's past medical history has been remarkably insignificant, with only a 20-kilo weight gain in the past three days.
- ✦ She slipped on the ice and apparently her legs went in separate directions in early December.
- ✦ The patient had a rash over his truck.
- ✦ She has had no rigors or shaking chills, but her husband states she was very hot in bed last night.
- ✦ Patient was released to outpatient department without dressing.
- ✦ I have suggested that he loosen his pants before standing, and then, when he stands with the help of his wife, they should fall to the floor.
- ✦ The patient has no past history of suicides.
- ✦ The patient experienced sudden onset of severe shortness of breath with a picture of acute pulmonary oedema at home while having sex, which gradually deteriorated in the emergency room.
- ✦ Patient has two teenage children, but no other abnormalities.
- ✦ Skin: somewhat pale but present.

## Dirty Wash

What do you do if someone's having a seizure in a swimming pool?

Throw in your dirty clothes!

## Daffy Definitions

- ✦ Constipation: To have and to hold.
- ✦ Hypochondriac: Someone who takes different pills than you do.
- ✦ Hypocrite: Someone who complains about sex, drugs and violence on their VCR.
- ✦ Costrophobia: Fear of rising drug prices.
- ✦ Credit card disease: Spendicitus.

## What is…

What is the proper medical term for circumcision of a rabbit?

A Hare Cut!

What is 18 inches long and hangs in front of an a\*\*\*hole?

A stethoscope!

What is the difference between a haematologist and a urologist?

A haematologist pricks your finger.

# Short Medical Insights

## The History of Medicine

2000 BC. Here, eat this root.

1000 AD. That root is heathen. Here, say this prayer.

1850 AD. That prayer is superstition. Here, drink this potion.

1940 AD. That potion is snake oil. Here, swallow this pill.

1985 AD. That pill is ineffective. Here, take this antibiotic.

2000 AD. That antibiotic is artificial. Here, eat this root.

## Smoker's Bumper Draw

Poster on a school notice board for a no-smoking campaign:

Good News For All Smokers!

The International Tobacco Syndicate, on its Golden Anniversary, wishes to invite Smokers of all ages to join in its biggest Anniversary Bumper Prize Draw, where every smoker is a sure winner! All smokers have the chance of winning the following major prizes.

Grand Prizes: A Brand New Cancer, Bronchial Infection, Goitre, Sinusitis, Migraine, Cerebral Tumour, Paralysis, Hypertension, and Asthma.

Second Prizes: Special Hepatitis, Meningitis, Bronchitis.

Third Prizes: Collared TB, Emphysema, Arteriosclerosis, Gingivitis, Rheumatism, Heart Disease, and Lung Cancer.

You can also have a chance to win consolation prizes such as: Tartar Deposits, Bad Breath, Stained Teeth, Appetite Loss, and Swelled Gums.

Join now!!! Remember that the more sticks you puff, the more chances of easy winning. Fabulous prizes await you!!! You can also be a lucky winner! Please claim your prizes at the nearest funeral parlour.

This promo is a limited offer.

See your X-Ray result for more details!!!

## 10-Point code of ethical behaviour for patients:

1. Do not expect your doctor to share your discomfort. Involvement with the patient's suffering might cause him to lose valuable scientific objectivity.

2. Be cheerful at all times. Your doctor leads a busy and trying life and requires all the gentleness and reassurance he can get.

3. Try to suffer from the disease for which you are being treated. Remember that your doctor has a professional reputation to uphold.

4. Do not complain if the treatment fails to bring relief. You must believe that your doctor has achieved a deep insight into the true nature of your illness, which transcends any mere permanent disability you may have experienced.

5. Never ask your doctor to explain what he is doing or why he is doing it. It is presumptuous to assume that such profound matters could be explained in terms that you would understand.

6. Submit to novel experimental treatment readily. Though the surgery may not benefit you directly, the resulting research paper will surely be of widespread scientific interest.

7. Pay your medical bills promptly and willingly. You should consider it a privilege to contribute, however modestly, to the well-being of physicians and other humanitarians.

8. Do not suffer from ailments that you cannot afford. It is sheer arrogance to contract illnesses that are beyond your means.

9. Never reveal any of the shortcomings that have come to light in the course of treatment by your doctor. The patient-doctor relationship is a privileged one and you have a sacred duty to protect him from exposure.

10. Never die while in your doctor's presence or under his direct care. This will only cause him needless inconvenience and embarrassment.

## The Story of Childbirth

Two different theories exist concerning the origin of children: the theory of sexual reproduction, and the theory of the stork.

Many people believe in the theory of sexual reproduction because they have been taught this theory at school. In reality, however, many of the world's leading scientists are in favour of the theory of the stork. If the theory of sexual reproduction is taught in schools, it must only be taught as a theory and not as the truth.

Alternative theories, such as the theory of the stork, must also be taught. Evidence supporting the theory of the stork includes the following:

1. It is a scientifically established fact that the stork does exist. This can be confirmed by every ornithologist.

2. The alleged human foetal development contains several features that the theory of sexual reproduction is unable to explain.

3. The theory of sexual reproduction implies that a child is approximately nine months old at birth. This is an absurd claim. Everyone knows that a newborn child is newborn!

4. According to the theory of sexual reproduction, children are a result of sexual intercourse. There are, however, several well-documented cases where sexual intercourse has not led to the birth of a child.

5. Statistical studies in the Netherlands have indicated a positive correlation between the birth rate and the number of storks. Both are decreasing.

6. The theory of the stork can be investigated by rigorous scientific methods. The only assumption involved is that children are delivered by the stork.

# Doctored Rhyme

From What The Queen Said by Stoddard King:

The Doctors

Nowadays there's little meaning
For a person to be gleaning
When a man attaches "Doctor" to his name
He may be a chiropractor
Or a painless tooth extractor
He's entitled to the title just the same.

Or perhaps he is a preacher
Or a lecturer or teacher,
Or an expert who cures chickens of the pip;
He may keep a home for rummies,
Or massage fat people's tummies,
Or specialise in ailments of the hip.

Everybody is a "Doctor",
From the backwoods herb concocter

To the man who takes bunions from your toes;
From the frowning dietician
To the snappy electrician
Who shocks you loose from all the body's woes!
So there's very little meaning
For a sufferer to be gleaning
When a man attaches "Doctor" to his name.
He may pound you, he may starve you,
He may cut your hair or carve you,
You have got to call him "Doctor" all the same!

## Makkar's Kidney Stone

It had to happen sooner or later. Lawyer Makkar was wheeled into the emergency room on a stretcher, rolling his head in agony.

Doctor Tejpal came over to see him. "Makkar," he said. "What an honour. The last time I saw you was in court when you accused me of malpractice."

"Doc! Doc! My side is on fire. The pain is right here. What could it be?"

"How would I know? You told the judge I wasn't fit to be a doctor."

"I was only kidding, doc. When you represent a client you don't know what you're saying. Could I be passing a kidney stone?"

"Your diagnosis is as good as mine."

"What are you talking about?"

"When you questioned me in the box you indicated you knew everything there was to know about the practice of medicine."

"Doc, I'm climbing the wall. Give me something."

"Let's say I give you something for a kidney stone and it turns out to be a gallstone. Who is going to pay for my court costs?"

"I'll sign a paper that I won't sue."

"Can I read to you from the transcript of the trial? Lawyer Makkar: 'Why were you so sure that my client had tennis elbow?' Dr Tejpal: 'I've treated hundreds of people with tennis elbow and I know it, when I see it.' Makkar: 'It never occurred to you my client could have a migraine headache?' Tejpal: 'No, there were no signs of a migraine headache.' Makkar: 'You and your ilk make me sick.'"

"Why are you reading that to me?"

"Because, Makkar, since the trial I've lost confidence in making a diagnosis. A lady came in the other day limping..."

"Please, doc, I don't want to hear it now. Give me a painkiller."

"You said during the suit that I dispensed drugs like a drunken sailor. I've changed my ways, Makkar. I don't prescribe drugs anymore."

"Then get me another doctor."

"There are no other doctors on duty. The reason I'm here is that after the malpractice suit the Police Commissioner seized everything in my office. This is the only place where I can practise."

"If you give me something to relieve the pain I will personally appeal your case to a higher court."

"You know, Makkar, I was sure that you were a prime candidate for a kidney stone."

"You can't tell a man is a candidate for a kidney stone just by looking at him."

"That's what you think, Makkar. You had so much acid in you when you addressed the judge I knew some of it eventually had to crystallise into stones. Remember on the third day when you called me the 'Butcher of Operating Room 6'? That afternoon I said to my wife, 'That man is going to be in a lot of pain.'"

"Okay, doc, you've had your ounce of flesh. Can I now have my ounce of a painkiller?"

"I better check you out first."

"Don't check me out, just give me the painkiller."

"But in court the first question you asked me was if I had examined the patient completely. It would be negligent of me if I didn't do it now. Do you mind getting up on the scale?"

"What for?"

"To find out your height. I have to be prepared in case I get sued and the lawyer asks me if I knew how tall you were."

"I'm not going to sue you."

"You say that now. But how can I be sure you won't file a writ after you pass the kidney stone?"

## Practical Psychoanalysis

Sigmund Freud had many interesting things to say about people's attitudes to laundry. Here is a quick test to see how you relate to it:

When watching your clothes going round in the tumble drier, what do you look out for?

A) Jeans B) Shirts C) Socks D) Sex

What frightens you most about going into the laundrette?

A) Losing one sock of your favourite pair
B) Putting whites and colours together so the colours mix
C) Spiders
D) Sex

What do you use to wash your clothes?

A) Surf B) Nirma C) Ariel D) Bio-Sex

You see a coffee stain on one of your shirts. What does it remind you of?

A) Someone you know
B) Coffee
C) A butterfly
D) Sex

If you answered D to most of these questions and coincidentally belong to the fairer sex, then I would be most interested in meeting you in person and discussing it at greater length – and in depth.

## Kinsey & Kinky Facts

Kinsey Report: Sexual Behaviour In The Human Male – 98% of males (including married men) admitted to masturbating. Average: 3 times per week.

And, 85% admitted premarital sex; 50% admitted adultery (Kinsey, et al. 1948).

Current adult male population in the United States = 134,349,027.

## Assumption

It takes at least ten minutes (on average) for a man to masturbate.

## The Calculations

134,349,027 men in the United States x 3 wack-offs/week = 403,047,081 wack-offs/week

6 ten-minute-periods/hour x 24 hours/day x 7 days/week = 1,008 ten-minute-periods/week

403,047,081 wack-offs/week/1,008 ten-minute-periods/week = 399,848 wack-offs/ten-minute-period

399,848 wack-offs/ten-minute-period x 98% (Kinsey Factor) = 391,851 wack-offs/ten-minute-period

## Conclusion

At any given moment (on average), 391,851 men in the United States are wacking-off.

So... be careful whom you shake hands with when you're in the United States!

# The Ultimate Medical Glossary

## Taxonomy of Medical Professions
- An acher of bacteriologists
- A murmur of cardiologists
- A stain of cytotechnologists
- A rash of dermatologists
- A speck of forensic pathologists
- A poke of gynaecologists
- A vessel of heart surgeons
- A clot of haematologists
- A nursery of obstetricians
- A dose of pharmacists
- A pile of proctologists
- A G-spot of sex therapists
- A stream of urologists

## The Moron's Glossary of Medical Terms

| | | |
|---|---|---|
| Anti-Body | = | Against everyone |
| Artery | = | Study of paintings |
| Bacteria | = | Back door to a cafeteria |
| Bandages | = | The Rolling Stones |
| Barium | = | What doctors do when treatment fails! |

| | | |
|---|---|---|
| Benign | = | What you be after you be eight! |
| Botulism | = | Tendency to make mistakes |
| Bowel | = | A letter like A, E, I, O, or U |
| Caesarean Section | = | A district in Rome |
| Cardiac Arrest | = | Going to jail |
| Cardiology | = | Advanced study of poker playing |
| Catarrh | = | Stringed instrument |
| Cat Scan (1) | = | Searching for kitty |
| Cat Scan (2) | = | What dogs do when they enter your yard |
| Cauterise | = | Make eye contact with the nurse |
| Colic | = | A sheep dog |
| Coma | = | A punctuation mark |
| Congenital | = | Friendly |
| Cortisone | = | The local courthouse |
| Cyst | = | To strongly urge |
| Dilate | = | To live long |
| Doctor | = | Having put a ship into dock |
| Enema | = | Not a friend |
| Enteritis | = | A penchant for burglary |
| Fester | = | Quicker |
| Fibrillate | = | To tell lies |
| Fibula | = | Small lie |
| Flu | = | Going by airplane |
| Genes | = | Blue denim slacks |
| Genital | = | Not Jewish |
| Haemorrhoid | = | A male from outer space |
| Hangnail | = | Coat hook |
| Heart | = | Injured |
| Herpes | = | What women do in the Ladies Room |
| Hormones | = | What a prostitute does when she doesn't get paid |
| ICU | = | Peek-a-boo |

| | | |
|---|---|---|
| Inpatient | = | Tired of waiting |
| Impotent | = | Distinguished; well known |
| Labour Pain | = | Getting hurt at work |
| Lung | = | Hope for intently |
| Medical Staff | = | Doctor's cane |
| Morbid | = | Higher bid |
| Nitrate | = | Cheaper than a day rate |
| Node | = | Was aware of |
| Organ transplant | = | What you do to your piano when you move |
| Organic | = | Organ repairman |
| Outpatient | = | Person who has fainted |
| Papsmear | = | Fatherhood test |
| Paralyse | = | Two far-fetched stories |
| Pathological | = | A reasonable way to go |
| Pelvis | = | Cousin of Elvis |
| Pharmacist | = | Person who makes a living dealing in agriculture |
| Post-operative | = | Letter carrier |
| Prostate | = | Flat on your back |
| Protein | = | In favour of young people |
| Recovery Room | = | Place to do upholstery |
| Rectum | = | Almost killed him |
| Rheumatic | = | Amorous |
| Saline | = | Where you go on your boyfriend's boat |
| Secretion | = | Hiding something |
| Seizure | = | Roman emperor |
| Serology | = | Study of English knighthood |
| Staph | = | Co-workers or employees |
| Strep | = | To disrobe |
| Suture | = | To satisfy |
| Tablet | = | A small table |
| Terminal Illness | = | Getting sick at the airport |

| | | |
|---|---|---|
| Tibia | = | Country in North Africa |
| Tumour | = | More than one |
| Ultrasound | = | Auditory manifestation of an expensive stereo system |
| Urine | = | Opposite of "You're Out" |
| Varicose | = | Near by |
| Vein | = | Conceited |
| X-ray | = | Eliminate Ray from the schedule |

❏❏❏

www.ingramcontent.com/pod-product-compliance
Lightning Source LLC
Chambersburg PA
CBHW070333230426
43663CB00011B/2294